The
Bicycle
Commuter's
Handbook

– – **Gear You Need** – –

– – **Clothes to Wear** – –

– – **Tips for Traffic** – –

– – **Roadside Repair** – –

ROBERT HURST

D1022903

FALCONGUIDES

GUILFORD, CONNECTICUT
HELENA, MONTANA

AN IMPRINT OF GLOBE PEQUOT PRESS

FALCONGUIDES®

All interior photos are by the author unless otherwise noted.

Project Editor: Lynn Zelem
Text Design: Maggie Peterson
Layout Artist: Melissa Evarts

Library of Congress Cataloging-in-Publication Data is available on file.

ISBN 978-0-7627-8468-4

Printed in the United States of America
10 9 8 7 6 5 4 3 2 1

Contents

PART III: The Ride

PART IV: At Work

PART V: Routine Maintenance

Introduction:
Bike Commuting on the Rise

North America has never been a bicycle commuter's paradise.

Even before the automobile, at a time when bicycling was a new, exciting, and wildly popular trend, there wasn't too much bike commuting going on. There were hordes of bicyclists on the roads—almost entirely for recreational purposes. As the advantages of utility cycling became obvious and many different types of no-nonsense bicyclists appeared (like police, line inspectors, mail carriers, and messengers), commuting to work by bike somehow failed to catch fire. Perhaps this was due to the effectiveness of the rail services at the time.

Three-quarters of a century later, adult bicycling rose again. In the 1960s elements of the European bicycle racing culture began to infiltrate North America, and after the first oil crisis of the 1970s, we had a full-blown fad on our hands. (More adult bicycles were sold in 1973 than any year before or since, according to the Bicycle Dealers' Association.) These bikes had skinny tires and, as far as most Americans were concerned, funny-looking handlebars. Many people began to ride their "ten-speeds" to work or class, especially in college towns like Davis and Boulder. At the same time, bicycling by kids was flourishing. School bike racks were full. American cities began to install various forms of cycling infrastructure. The future of bike commuting was looking very bright.

Then of course America doubled down on driving for a few decades. This was a complex time for bike commuting and bicycling in general. Gas was cheap again in the United States after the crises of the 1970s dissolved. Vehicles were super-size, and families moved way out into the suburbs, and then to the suburbs of the suburbs. Cheap credit for cars and houses was the name of the game. But important developments kept the idea of the bike floating around our frontal lobes during these decades of driving as a core group of die-hard commuters continued pedaling to work. In 1982 the first production mountain bikes arrived in shops. Fat-tired bikes captured the imagination and caused an immense expansion of bike industry and culture. While this was happening, Greg Lemond climbed the lofty pinnacle of the Tour de France, winning the race three times and sending a new generation of American kids onto the roads with peloton daydreams. By the end of the century, American racers were dominant in European racing behind seven-time Tour winner Lance Armstrong. Armstrong and his compatriots have been exposed as liars, and the public has come to realize that doping and pro cycling are inextricably linked. It remains to be seen what effect, if any, this new understanding will have on our cycling renaissance.

In the late 2000s the credit bubble burst and the specter of expensive fuel reemerged, not necessarily in that order. The number of bike commuters spiked along with gas prices. From coast to coast, city governments stoked the fires by adding Euro-inspired bike infrastructure and "bike share" programs. Cities like Portland, San Francisco, and New York saw huge increases in the numbers of bicyclists, commuters included. According to the US Census Bureau, the number of frequent bicycle commuters in the thirty-eight largest "bicycle-friendly communities" grew by 77 percent between 2000 and 2010. (The term "bicycle-friendly community" comes from "2010 Bicycle Commuting Data Released," a report by the League of American Bicyclists.)

The near doubling of bike commuters in these cities is impressive, but it seems less so when you consider that we're talking about a hike from 0.8 percent to 1.4 percent. The overall average for the United States is even less impressive. While the national average has also improved a lot, it remains in the neighborhood of 0.5 percent. In other words, you need to line up 200

American workers before you find *one* who commutes by bike. And that's a major improvement.

But today that one person is you, so it is cause for celebration.

THE COSTS AND BENEFITS OF COMMUTING BY BIKE

I started bike commuting for two simple reasons: to get a little exercise and so the people at work would think I was hard core.

—Giles Clasen

What can bike commuting do for you? Other than completely change your life, not much.

One benefit of commuting by bicycle is saving money—saving a great deal of money, in fact, if you are able to wave good-bye to car ownership entirely, jettisoning insurance and registration fees along with fuel and maintenance costs. Admittedly, if you keep a car, there is much less to be saved by riding a bike to work. Some bike commuters find that money saved on gasoline and parking is largely offset by copious bike-related purchases, leaving them about the same as before in terms of money.

While you may not save a pile of cash commuting by bike, there are still more powerful benefits to be gained. The bicycle is the most efficient vehicle known to man, an important consideration in these interesting times. Bicycle commuters require energy to move themselves—but not nearly as much as they would expend using a motor vehicle. When bicycling to work, you're likely to burn energy at a rate roughly equivalent to 1,000 miles per gallon! Using such an efficient mode of travel benefits the whole of society. Not only that, but you're spewing a lot less poison into the air and taking up a lot less space than your motorized counterparts. So thanks.

Exercise is probably the most important personal benefit of bike commuting. Moderately strenuous bicycling is fantastic exercise, and exercise is essential. Sitting behind the wheel of a car is the opposite of good exercise. It was no surprise when a study published in the June 2012 issue of *American Journal of Preventive Medicine* found that car commuters suffer cardiovascular health problems at a rate directly related to the length of their commutes. In sharp contrast, the longer your bike commute, the better off you are likely to be.

Let's face it. To many people the exercise is not a positive but belongs on the other side of the ledger. Nothing will convince them otherwise. Bicycling probably isn't the best choice for folks who detest physical activity, although they may enjoy a motorized bike.

Another apparent cost of commuting by bike is time. Bike commuters usually have to leave earlier, sometimes a lot earlier than their motorized counterparts, and they arrive home later in the evening. But look a little closer. Bike commuters are exercising—effectively—at the same time they are transporting themselves to work. Imagine an hour-long bike commute that would take 30 minutes in a car. The cyclist spends an extra hour in travel but gets 2 hours' worth of good exercise while commuting. If we look at it this way, then the bike commuter comes out ahead. To complete the same trip and get 2 hours of exercise, the motorized commuter must spend 3 hours total—and he or she won't experience the fun and adventure of traveling by bicycle. Of course, given the time constraints, the motorist is unlikely to exercise at all.

Is bicycling more dangerous than driving? That would be an important cost. Well, we've just seen how driving is dangerous. It steadily destroys the health of those who do it. But bicycling is probably more likely to result in some sort of injury. Being on two wheels introduces an entirely different set of ways to injure oneself. Most cyclist injuries are minor and result from solo wipe-outs—things drivers don't have to worry about. When there is a collision, the unprotected bicyclist is less likely to escape unscathed.

But drivers have their own unique set of dangers when they get out onto the freeway or otherwise travel at speeds much higher than a bicyclist can reach on flat land. The unique dangers of bicycling translate into minor abrasions; the unique dangers of driving can result in serious or fatal injuries. Even without factoring in the health benefit of bicycling, any apparent safety advantage for driving would be tenable at best.

Bike commuters reap colossal benefits—fun, adventure, and huge improvements in mental and physical health—that overwhelm the costs. It's no wonder that so many bike commuters look back at their choice to start riding to work as one of the best choices they ever made.

PART I:
Equipment and Clothing

WHICH BIKE TO USE?

Bike commuters can use just about any type of bicycle successfully—and there are a lot of different types. Here are some of them, with some of the advantages and disadvantages associated with each. Personal preferences, priorities, and circumstances will determine which of these choices will be best for you.

Mountain bike. Introduced to the public in 1982, the machine ostensibly designed for use on mountain trails has become one of the most popular types of bicycles for commuting. The advantages and disadvantages of the mountain bike are outsized and obvious. They're sturdy on rough roads, tough, and good in the snow. But they're also heavier and slower. Suspension forks are counterproductive on the street. The same could be said for the fat, knobby tires that work so well off-road.

Perhaps the biggest advantage of mountain bikes is that a lot of people have them lying around the garage collecting dust—so no need to buy a new bike. To improve an old mountain bike for city use, exchange the knobby tires for slicks or semi-slicks, and try to set the bike up so it fits well for road use.

A lot of newer mountain bikes have 700c wheels (the same rim circumference as a road bike), noticeably larger than traditional "26-inch" mountain bike wheels. Called "29ers," these bikes may be better suited for road riding than bikes with smaller wheels.

Touring bike. With racks and fenders, the humble touring bike could very well be the most practical of all possible commuting bikes. Touring bikes are built for hauling a lot of weight over long distance, as well as for keeping the rider dry and comfortable. They're almost as rugged as mountain bikes, but as they're designed for road use, they roll a bit easier. They tend to be relatively heavy, even without the bags, with sturdy steel frames.

If sporty handling isn't on your wish list of bike attributes, a touring bike could be just what you're looking for. However, will you be able to find one? True touring bikes seem to be getting more and more rare as the years go by.

Road-racing bike. The road-racing bike offers the speediest, most efficient travel on pavement. It also has lively handling characteristics and may feel unstable or twitchy if you're not used to it. Road bikes are relatively light, but they're not fragile. Even the lightest among them, the true racing machines, are

This touring bike is outfitted with full fenders, rack, heavy-duty wheels and tires—and weighs about 800 pounds.

built to withstand high speeds and racing conditions that could very well be more taxing and intense than your commute. However, problems can arise when larger people try to use racing equipment, or when commuters try to put a lot of weight on a featherweight bike. Carrying a significant amount of anything while riding such a bike may require the use of a backpack, since true racing bikes don't have fittings for easy installation of a rack. Racing bikes also tend to be quite expensive—a serious consideration, because any bike is more vulnerable to theft, vandalism, and frame-destroying collision in rough city environments at rush hour. But several manufacturers do offer good-quality road bikes for modest cost. Many commuters find either a dedicated racing machine or a bike patterned on one to be the most *fun* choice for commuting. Whether using such a bike is a wise choice is always up for debate. Honestly, much will depend on the local weather patterns.

An expensive racing bike that has been used as a commuter shows the signs of daily use in all weather. The bike's frame and components are racy, but durable.

Hybrid. The hybrid is hard to define. Ostensibly it is a cross between a mountain bike and a road bike. Hybrids tend to be outfitted with suspension forks and flat bars—the attributes of mountain bikes associated with comfort—but are not rugged enough to be used on rough trails. The advantages and disadvantages are clear. These bikes are comfortable and generally affordable, easy to operate, and easy to outfit with typical commuting equipment. The features that attract beginners, such as the shocks and flat-resistant tires, also make the bike more difficult to propel down the road.

Comfort bike. The so-called "comfort bike" is a hybrid with even more squishy features, such as a suspension seat post, wide seat, and high handlebars. Trade-offs abound.

Folding bike. A folding bike is designed especially for commuters and travelers. Built with small wheels, these bikes can be carried like luggage when folded. This is a great feature for commuters who take the train or bus for part of their trip. Even though public transit systems have made good headway with carrying passengers' bikes, a folding bike will still be easier in many situations. The trade-off, as you might imagine, is that these little wheels don't roll quite as easily or as comfortably as their 700c cousins. Gearing can become an issue as well, because the "size" of the gear decreases with wheel size.

Cyclocross bikes. Cyclocross is a form of bike racing born long ago in the dismal off-seasons of northern Europe. Dedicated cyclocross bikes have been adopted for all kinds of non-racing purposes. These bikes look like regular road bikes at first glance, but they tend to have beefier wheels and tires, much heavier frames, and cantilever brakes. They are designed to continue operating in the muck, which could be a helpful feature.

Single-speed. Just about any kind of bike could be made into a single-speed, and some start out that way. Single-speed bikes have almost all the features of other bikes, except the extra gears. Riding a single-speed is not as disadvantageous as you might assume. Derailleurs and cogs weigh a significant amount.

Ditching them makes for a lighter and more maneuverable machine and leaves you with a lot less to think about while riding—and a lot less to fix or maintain when not riding. Of course choosing one gear will result in the occasional stretches where that gear doesn't match the terrain as well as you'd like. If your commute is on relatively flat land, however, one well-chosen gear is all you really need.

Fixed-gear. A subset of single-speed bikes, the fixed-gear is distinguished by its lack of a freewheel. This means the fixed-gear bike can't coast—the pedals are turning whenever the wheel is turning. A rider can slow a fixed-gear with backward pressure on the pedals but can't stop as quickly as one can with a freewheel and brakes. This becomes a serious safety issue for riders who don't really know what they're doing. Some riders prefer the sense of being completely connected to the bike through the drivetrain. Typically, fixed-gear bikes are pure track-racing bikes that have been kidnapped for road use, or old road bikes that have been rescued and modified. It's possible, but not recommended, to ride a fixed-gear without handbrakes.

A single-speed bike equipped with a freewheel and two handbrakes.

Recumbent. The recumbent offers a completely different position than a diamond-framed bike. On the recumbent the rider reclines in a low "chair" with a back; the feet and crankset are at the front of the bike. This position is more aerodynamic and arguably safer in the event of a wipeout. For medical reasons, it may be the only position in which some people can ride. Recumbent bikes can be very comfortable and efficient on long, flat stretches of road. And *fast*. Recumbent bikes with full fairings—and powered by world-class pedalers—have reached speeds over 80 miles per hour!

The disadvantages of recumbents quickly become apparent on climbs and in tight, urban areas. Recumbent riders can't stand on the pedals, have more difficulty maneuvering the machine around obstacles, can't hop curbs, and can't easily carry their much heavier machine up a flight of stairs, for instance. In city traffic the rider on the lower recumbent may be even easier to overlook than an upright cyclist. For the commuter, any one of these disadvantages could be a deal-breaker.

Cruiser. It's certainly possible to commute on a cruiser: an old-fashioned bike outfitted with coaster brakes, a huge cushy

Cruisers are among the most fashionable, and least efficient, bikes for commuting.

seat, very wide handlebars and tires, and, if you're lucky, a three-speed transmission. It's an extremely casual setup. Many commuters ride cruisers to work successfully and happily, but happy cruiser commutes are almost always very short.

Electric. Is a motorized bicycle still a bicycle? This philosophical question is currently being ignored by millions of happy users of bikes with battery-powered electric-assist motors. Such "e-bikes" have become very popular with commuters in recent years. Although this boom has occurred primarily in parts of the world far removed from the North American bike scene, it seems to be on its way to a multiuse path near you. (Should motorized bikes be allowed on nonmotorized paths? That's another question for another day.)

The electric bikes currently available for retail sale in North America are usually cheap or medium-quality bikes with a battery-powered motor attached. The motor assist is usually not super powerful and the bikes are almost always very heavy to begin with. On hills the motor may provide just enough boost to make the incline seem like flat land. For this you will pay a hefty premium at the shop or, ever more likely, when buying online.

Critics of e-bikes point not only to high prices that are not justified for mediocre-quality equipment but also to the negative consequences of motorized assistance. Installing a motor neutralizes the bicycle's special advantage over other forms of commuter transportation: Bicycling is especially good exercise; riding a motorized bike is not. But one man's critique is another's advertisement.

Bike share bikes. Residents of many cities are enjoying new "bike share" programs, and many more will in the future. These public-private programs aren't really about "sharing." They are semi-subsidized rental schemes, designed to make bikes available for short trips around town. Although they weren't necessarily put in place for commuters, these fleets are being used for daily commutes by people who are lucky enough to live and work close to the kiosks where the bikes are

Bike share bikes are as heavy as boat anchors. They are also among the toughest, most reliable bikes on the road. Savvy commuters know how the local system works and where the fleet bikes are located so that they can be used in a pinch.

rented and returned. The advantages of using such a bike are obvious. First of all, it's a lot cheaper than buying a new bike if you don't have one. And since the bike isn't yours, you don't have to worry about maintenance or replacing worn-out components. Outfitted with full fenders and drum brakes, they are also good bikes for wet weather. Disadvantages are obvious too. These machines are terribly heavy, since they are built as sturdy as possible. They are hard to move, and top speeds are relatively low. But lugging one of these anchors around each day might be your new training secret.

FRAME MATERIALS

Most of the more affordable bikes these days have frames made of aluminum. These frames, which tend to be mass-produced in China, provide reliable service at a reasonable weight and a relatively low cost. They work. Repairability is the downfall of aluminum, however. If you crash hard and crack or bend the frame, its days are usually done.

There are many different types of steel tubing and methods for welding it together. Steel frames can be relatively cheap and heavy (and, like most aluminum frames, made in highly automated Asian factories), or very light and expensive, pieced together by hand in some small shop. The belief that light steel frames provide ideal ride qualities—giving just enough for comfort over the bumps while retaining a lively feel—has been particularly resilient in cycling mythology. The belief survives because it rings true to a lot of riders. Furthermore, a bent steel frame can often be forced back into alignment with no long-term ill effects. The repairability of steel is supreme. Steel frames have gone up in the esteem of bike people everywhere, and, cause-and-effect, so has their price.

Titanium is similar to steel but is lighter, more difficult to work with, and even more expensive. Not all titanium frames are the same by any means, and titanium tubing, as well as frame fabrication, spans a wide range in terms of quality.

Good quality bikes almost always have a sticker displaying the brand and type of tubing used to make the frame.

The latest common frame material to appear is carbon fiber. Carbon frames can be made very, very light while remaining impressively tough. The Tour de France peloton, which for many years raced on a mix of steel, aluminum, and titanium frames, is now 100 percent carbon equipped. An expensive carbon frame may not be the best choice for commuting if the commute will involve adverse conditions, and, perhaps more important, the bike could get roughed up during locking and storage. That said, I'm certain that there are many commuters out there using carbon bikes and loving every minute of it. Expect more advanced, affordable carbon frames to come on the market as the technology improves.

BIKE FIT

No matter which sort of bike you end up with, how it fits you will determine how much you enjoy riding it, how fast you can pedal, and for how long. The fit will have great influence on your ability to turn, stop, or perform the nifty bike trick of your choice. Fit is extremely important. Poor fit will undermine the enjoyability of the ride and actually could cause injury.

Unfortunately there are few universal formulas that can be trotted out for beginners to use when setting up a bike. (There are some formulas, but they are forever up for debate, so hardly universal.) Bike fit is necessarily somewhat subjective. The needs of each individual are different because individuals' bodies are different. But there are some basic parameters that you want to remain within, no matter what type of bike you're using, because the consequences of going too far can actually be serious. Many of the "overuse" injuries associated with cycling are really caused by poor fit.

If you're in the market for a new or used bike, make sure you get one with a frame size in the right range for your height. Standover height is the most *immediate* concern: When you step off the seat, the height of the top tube (the horizontal frame tube connecting the seat tube to the front of the bike) must be lower than the height of your crotch. Otherwise, there could be painful occurrences. (For road use you'll be able to get away with riding a taller bike than would be advisable off-road, but standover is still an important consideration.)

Beyond that first simple requirement, the frame can be within a fairly large range of length and height and still work. Although the ultimate length and height of your setup will be somewhat adjustable—a longish top tube can be corrected with a shorter stem, a smaller frame might work with a long seat post, etc.—there are limits to how far an off-size frame can be pushed. It's best to start with a frame that fits well.

Assuming you're starting with a frame size that is in the right ballpark, start to dial in the fit by adjusting the seat height, seat fore-aft, and seat angle. Seat height should be set so that the legs retain a little bit of a bend at the bottom of the pedal stroke but not so high that the hips rock during pedaling. You shouldn't need to reach at all with your hips, feet, or ankles when the pedals pass closest to the ground.

The saddle (a more accurate term than "seat," although it sounds a bit snobbish) is an often misunderstood piece of equipment. Think of it not so much as a place upon which to plop all your weight but as a sort of perch to prop yourself up. Remember, more weight should be on the pedals than the seat. Depending on specific preferences, pedaling styles, and body types, the saddle can be positioned forward or back several centimeters on the seat post. For optimal pedaling, when the cranks are parallel to the ground, an imaginary plumb line dropped from the front of the forward knee should hit the top of the foot over the pedal axle, roughly speaking. The angle of the seat can be set as well. Keep it level with the ground or tipped down slightly in front. (The more seated climbing you do, the more sense a tipped-down saddle will make.) I recommend not pointing the saddle up toward the sky, as this seems to lead to reproductive issues and discomfort in both men and women.

Combined with "clipless" pedals, cleats like this give commuters more power and control (not at the office, on the bike). They can be a little tricky to set up correctly—and can cause painful problems if they're not.

If you're using "clipless" pedals, take some care in setting up the cleats. Don't set the angle too far away from straight (parallel to the crank arm). Fixing the cleats too far forward or back on the shoe could lead to knee problems. Start with a centered position, and make minute adjustments as preferences emerge. If the cleat comes loose, it could change position slightly and start causing problems. Similarly, a worn-out cleat might mess with the pedaling motion and cause knee pain in addition to other problems.

The height of the handlebars can be adjusted by using stems of different angles, and sometimes by moving the stem up or down on the steer tube. (Sometimes the steer tube has been cut down, removing this possibility.) The fore-aft position of the hands can be adjusted with stems of different lengths. Handlebar position is important for the feel of the bike. In terms of preventing repetitive injury, it's not as critical as seat height but will still cause some problems if it's badly botched.

Handlebar height has become a culturally charged issue within one contingent of our diverse bicycling community. Many seem to equate high handlebars with comfortable cycling. A cloud of misunderstanding hangs around the whole issue. High handlebars necessitate a very upright riding position, which certainly has its charms. For short rides in urban traffic, it works well. Just think of those throngs of daily commuters in Holland and Denmark. This is a more natural position for beginning riders. But sitting bolt upright on a bike means that almost all your weight is on the seat. *But wait,* you may be asking yourself, *isn't that where it's supposed to be?* In fact, no. For optimal comfort on a bike, your weight should be distributed over the feet, the arms and hands, and the sit bones (ischial tuberosities). If it helps you achieve this balanced position, lowering the handlebars a bit will not sacrifice your comfort to the evil consumerist forces of sport cycling after all.

The handlebars might be several inches lower than seat height and still provide a comfortable position. When the handlebars are clearly below the saddle, it might look very uncomfortable to the uninitiated. Many assume this must be an aggressive racing position. In reality this is just the way it works out due to our strange-looking human forms. With the handlebars below the seat, the long-armed human can still ride in a casual, upright position; in an aggressive, low position; or anything in between. Because it releases a bit of weight from the rear end, this could be the only handlebar position that allows the rider to pedal for long distances in comfort.

Aerodynamics are also an important factor in bicycling comfort, although we don't typically think of wind resistance as a comfort issue. The comfort of sitting upright can be nearly canceled by the extra wind resistance, which makes propelling the bike significantly more difficult. However, we can't say that the most aerodynamic position is the most comfortable—far from it. Pro racers work very hard on perfecting their most aerodynamic position for time-trialing, because it doesn't really come naturally. Luckily for everyday utility cyclists, the comfortable position that distributes the weight among the feet, hands, and seat is also reasonably aerodynamic. It's not perfect, but it could be a lot worse.

When it's all said and done, dialing in the position on the bike is a matter of adjusting two contact points (the handlebars/grips and the seat) in relation to a third (the pedal) to form an imaginary triangle.

Bad bike fit is one of the unnecessary obstacles keeping many from bicycling regularly. Unfortunately, a lot of the people who are being tyrannized by bad bike fit don't even realize it! They figure that bicycling just naturally causes pain in the knees or back or hands or crotch and there's not much they can do about it other than get used to it. Well, know this: Bicycling is not supposed to hurt, or even be significantly uncomfortable, in any of the aforementioned body locations. If cycling feels painful and wrong, there's most likely some fit issue causing the problem.

TROUBLESHOOTING BIKE FIT

The following are some common bike-related ailments and their possible relation to bike fit—or, more accurately, misfit:

Knee pain. If the pain is at the front of the knee, the seat could be too low. If the pain is at the back of the knee, the seat could be too high. Knee pain is also caused by bad pedaling motion, worn-out cleats and shoes, or poorly installed (i.e., misaligned) cleats. Take knee pain seriously. If you have to keep riding with knee pain, use an easy, spinning gear.

Numb or sore hands. Numb hands are a sign that you are putting too much weight on your hands. Generally this means the handlebars are too low. Raise and/or tilt them to ease the pressure and put a little more weight back on the rear. You shouldn't have to reach for the bars. Hold on with a relaxed grip and arms slightly bent.

Numbness in the crotch. This is a sign that you are putting too much weight on the seat, and in the wrong way. Often the culprit is a tilted-up saddle. Adjust the height and angle of the seat so that only the sit bones press against it. The soft tissue around the perineum and the various bits and pieces should be nearly free of pressure. Fix this issue immediately to avoid potential life-altering consequences. The common impulse to use a very soft saddle may do more harm than good, causing excess pressure between the sit bones, where it doesn't belong. Some minor discomfort in this region is normal for beginners or after a long layoff from cycling, but it should go away when you get used to riding, not get worse.

Pain in the hips. Hip pain is common among bicyclists and is often caused by setting the seat too high. This is one of the most serious mistakes you could make when setting up a bike. Usually this pain manifests off the bike, and it can become a debilitating medical issue if not addressed. Make sure the seat is low enough that you don't have to reach for the bottom of the pedal stroke and the hips don't rock when pedaling.

Sore neck. Normal cycling may cause a sore neck in newer riders who aren't yet used to holding their head up to look forward. However, neck soreness might be attributed to an overly bent-over riding position. Try raising the bars a little bit.

Lower back pain. The lower back can be strained painfully if you simply push too hard before you're ready for it—too large of a gear for too long. There may not be any misfit issue here, although lower back pain may also be associated with an incorrect seat adjustment.

PEDALS AND SHOES

It's interesting how these topics tie together. Pedals are a key topic. Once you start writing about pedals, it leads invariably to a discussion of shoes. Soon you may be taking on the whole philosophy of clothes for commuting.

Basic pedals like this can be used with any type of shoe.

You may commute with "flat pedals" or "platform pedals." These require no special shoes, although some types of shoes will probably be a lot more comfortable than others. Versatility is the name of the game here. You can use flat pedals and bicycling-specific shoes or flat pedals and, say, tap-dancing shoes.

A popular option is to use so-called clipless pedals (a decades-old name referring to the break from the toe clip paradigm of yesteryear) with a cycling shoe that has a stiff sole and a cleat hidden on the bottom. Mountain bike shoes have recessed cleats and are designed for walking around off the bike, which makes them very practical for utility cycling. The more affordable versions of these mountain bike shoes tend to be disguised as regular casual or hiking shoes, a popular feature. They are designed for use with clipless pedals but can be used with any pedal setup. The dedicated road shoe, on the other hand, will provide even more power for pedaling but has an exaggerated protuberance on the bottom and isn't designed for walking.

Road shoes require special road pedals that don't work with other types of shoes.

Do click-in (i.e., clipless) pedals really make it easier to pedal, or is that just marketing gimmickry? Yes, there is a noticeable increase in power when a well-fitting shoe is physically attached to a pedal, although this increase is most apparent when you're standing out of the saddle. Clipless pedals also make it much easier for novice riders to hop curbs and potholes. However, they take extra care to set up, and it takes a little time to get the hang of being attached to the bike. This becomes second nature soon enough, but beginners might fall over a few times before they figure out the release mechanism. Awkward! When it comes down to it, just about everyone who learns to use clipless pedals is glad he or she did.

This pedal combines a large platform pedal and a clipless pedal to create one versatile—and relatively heavy—piece of equipment.

Many commuters love to use pedals that appear and act like flat pedals, accommodating any sort of shoe and providing the support of a large platform, but which also have a click-in mechanism for use with cleated shoes. These practical pedals are in some ways the best of both worlds, but they're relatively heavy.

Another option is to use pedals with old-fashioned toe clips and straps, which are still widely available. As with bare flat pedals, toe clips allow the rider to commute in work shoes, or any sort of shoe—including work boots if the toe clip is large enough—and still gain some obvious ergonomic advantage in pedaling.

As you can see, there are several pedal-shoe combinations that can be used for commuting—from sleek road-racing shoes attached to dedicated road-racing pedals, to dress shoes on old-fashioned flat pedals, and many, many variations between. Ultimately, your choice of commuting shoes and pedals may very well be determined by your situation at the workplace as much as your personal preferences.

FENDERS

If you commute in your work clothes, fenders could be the most important part of your commuting gear. A traditional set of full fenders, like you'd see on a Dutch bike, will work best. They won't keep you from getting wet, but they may keep you from getting soaked. Most important, they keep grimy, oily road splatter off your clothing and equipment. It may be helpful to attach a rubber flap or something similar to the bottom of the front fender for even better coverage. Even with all that coverage, full fenders are still likely to leave you with wet shoes, so plan accordingly.

There are more slapdash fender options available. If your bike doesn't have eyelets, or you just want to make things easier, clip-on fenders are available. These do a good job of keeping rear tire spray off the backside. They tend not to work very

A snap-on fender provides substantial defense against backside spray, but if you're really serious about keeping road splatter off your clothes, go with full fenders.

well for front tire spray, which is more problematic because it moves around with the tire. There's no substitute for the traditional hard-mounted full fender if you want to keep your front side dry.

Fenders can also cause complications. They can catch on a shoe in a sharp turn. Snow can collect under a fender in quantities sufficient to keep the tire from moving, which usually amounts to an annoyance rather than a real hazard. In rare instances a bicycle might roll over a stick in such a way that the stick is thrown up and gets stuck on the fender strut, stopping the wheel and throwing the rider. I recommend fenders with safety fasteners that break loose should this stick scenario occur.

Keep in mind that racing bikes aren't built to accommodate full fenders. They don't have eyelets for ease of installation (of racks or fenders), and the clearance between tire, frame, and brakes doesn't allow for traditional full-coverage fenders anyway—the number-one argument against using racing bikes for commuting.

LIGHTS

North American commuters ride in the dark on a regular basis. Especially in winter, the lights come out. It's a good thing too. Riding in the dark without proper lighting is one of the most dangerous mistakes a cyclist can make; besides that, it's against the law almost everywhere. Many bike commuters, like motorcyclists, run lights during the day for extra visibility.

Taillight. First and foremost, get a flashing red taillight or two. Some brands are much brighter than others. The brighter the better when it comes to the "blinkie," in my opinion. If you have panniers, put a flashing taillight on the left side of the left pannier.

Headlight. The main purpose of the headlight is to make *you* visible to other road users. Secondarily, it provides some light to help you avoid objects or potholes in the darkness. Headlights can be mounted on the handlebars of any type of bike, on a helmet, or both.

This taillight shows marks from having been dropped on the street numerous times.

A good headlight will make you visible to other road users—if they happen to be looking in your direction, that is.

Modern bike lights tend to be equipped with multiple LED (light-emitting diode) bulbs. In general, the more affordable lights are powered by regular AA batteries and can still be purchased for less than $30. The brighter lights are usually equipped with rechargeable lithium-ion batteries and can run into the hundreds of dollars. There are some small, affordable lithium-ion battery lights available as well. Often they are charged via a USB (universal serial bus) connection, which makes them easy to recharge in an office setting. Some commuters still like the old-style generator-powered lights that are illuminated whenever the bike is moving; these are perhaps more reliable, but they exact a toll in rolling resistance. Almost all models have different brightness settings and can be set to flash or "strobe." Since the main purpose is to be seen rather than see, most riders will be able to commute successfully without a very expensive, super-bright headlight.

The brightness of lights is measured in "lumens." About 100 lumens is all you need to be seen, but 300 lumens or so will get you *really* seen—maybe even from space. In fact, high-quality bike lights are so impressively bright on their brightest settings that they may do more harm than good. Users of super-bright helmet-mounted units, especially, should take care not to blind the drivers upon whose eyes they depend!

- -

PRO TIP: **Batteries function extremely poorly in very cold weather. The light will dim, and battery life will be much shorter than usual. Don't leave the light on the bike outside; keep it in your front pocket or some other warm spot, and it will be ready to go when you need it.**

- -

REFLECTIVE GEAR

Use lots of reflective gear, in creative ways. Make sure it's on your clothes and shoes, any packs or panniers, and your bike. A good cycling jacket will have bright reflective strips sewn into it. Reflective tape on the spokes is especially eye-catching. Any decent bike shop will carry all kinds of reflective products. In the meantime, keep the reflectors that came with your bike, if any, clean and securely attached. For the ultimate in reflectivity, go with the full reflective vest.

Keep in mind that there is no silver bullet that will get you noticed by every driver all the time. The effectiveness of any reflective gear or light varies as the background changes. Besides that, drivers may not even be looking in your direction.

BELL

The law in your state most likely requires that you give an audible warning of some kind before passing pedestrians on a multiuse path. Law or no law, pedestrians really appreciate not getting their shirtsleeves blown off by cyclists zinging past without warning. The traditional spoken warning that bicyclists are known to give other bicyclists—"on your left"—yields unpredictable results when directed at pedestrians. The universally recognized bell seems to do the trick more consistently.

MIRROR

Given that bicyclists can turn their heads around, and also learn to use their hearing effectively to detect approaching traffic, mirrors could hardly be considered absolutely necessary for bicycling. Relatively few riders use them, but among those that do, you'll detect a strong devotion to this bit of safety equipment. Bicycling mirrors may attach to the handlebars, but the small models that attach to sunglasses or helmets are niftier. They are compact yet effective, once you learn how to aim the device and actually see what's showing on the tiny reflective surface. Both types of mirrors are prone to breaking under daily use.

Riders with mirrors are clued in to the approach of vehicles much earlier than riders who must rely on hearing and "shoulder checks," which makes for a somewhat safer ride and less nervous rider. Mirrors are especially helpful on two-lane highways and in heavy downtown traffic, where vehicle noise overwhelms riders' sense of hearing.

TOOLS

First and foremost are the tools required to fix a flat. Acquire them and carry them whenever you ride: a patch kit, at least two tire levers, and a pump. Don't try to get away with only carrying a CO2 injector and a few cartridges; use the CO2 if you want, but bring the pump as well. Similarly, if you like to use so-called glueless patches, I recommend carrying a traditional Rema brand or similar patch kit to back them up. It's always a good idea to carry an extra tube or two as well to further ensure your timely arrival at your place of employment.

In addition to the flat-fixing tools, carry a few common Allen wrenches and a spoke wrench. Lots of commuters carry a multitool, which includes those items plus a screwdriver and perhaps a small adjustable wrench and chain tool, all combined in a single device.

LOCK

The best-case scenario is you don't need to carry a lock at all. You might be able to bring your bike into your office, for instance. But most commuters aren't so lucky.

A single "U-lock" (sort of shaped like a U) will do the trick for most commuters in most locations. These locks are impressively expensive, far from invincible, and inconveniently heavy, but they remain the option of choice after replacing cable locks decades ago. Avoid cable-style locks unless the cable is very thick. Many cable locks can be snipped with bolt cutters or a pair of big gardening shears. Some can even be pulled apart by hand. If you value your bike, secure it with a U-lock. Even the best lock can be beaten by a determined thief, and U-locks can be thwarted in a variety of ways. Some old ones can be picked with ease, but the new generation seems more trustworthy.

RACK

A rack is strictly optional for most commuters but mandatory for those who want to use panniers (see below). A rack can be used in conjunction with panniers, with a "trunk bag" that fits on top, with both of these at once, or without any sort of luggage at all. Some like to use a bare rack with a bungee cord or two to carry things like jackets and locks. If you do this, make absolutely sure that whatever's on the rack can't sneak into the spokes.

THE GREAT PANNIERS VERSUS BACKPACK DEBATE

The easiest, quickest route to becoming an instant bike commuter is to grab the bike you already have and the backpack you've had since the ninth grade and go. It's a time-tested mode of travel. Don't be afraid of the backpack.

Some very devoted cycle commuters swear by their racks and panniers and insist this method is far superior. You might think panniers are overkill for commuting and are better suited to lengthy tours. If you're hauling a significant amount of material home from work, however, or picking up some groceries on the way home, using panniers is downright pleasant. Panniers carry the load on the bike rather than the rider, which lets the rider spend more energy on pedaling. Of course that makes the bike itself heavier, and the center of gravity of the bike-rider system much lower, which changes the handling characteristics in

Panniers have a cultlike following.

what many feel to be a negative fashion. Use of panniers also helps riders avoid the problem of a sweaty *backpack back*.

Panniers can be inexpensive, but the really nice waterproof models are pricy. (And don't forget to factor in the cost of the rack.)

It's difficult to pick a clear winner in the panniers versus backpack cage match. Like most of the commuter's equipment choices, it comes down to personal preferences.

MESSENGER BAGS

As a longtime messenger, I won't be advising any commuters to use messenger bags, although many do. These single-strap shoulder bags allow messengers to swing the bag around their neck to quickly remove items from or place them in the bag without taking it off. It's a wonderful feature if you're making lots of quick stops, constantly locking and unlocking the bike, and retrieving items from or placing them in the bag. If all you want to do is carry something from here to there, the messenger bag is not the best choice. At some point they become a liability, albeit a minor one. In fact, a lot of messengers now use special backpack-style messenger bags, sacrificing that old-school convenience for additional control and comfort while riding.

Bike commuters who have only tried messenger bags may not fully realize how nice backpacks are in comparison. Similarly, those who know backpacks alone may not be able to grasp the joy of a good set of panniers.

OTHER BIKE LUGGAGE AND BASKETS

While traditional panniers require a rack for mounting, there are all kinds of special bags available that can be mounted under the seat or on various parts of the frame and handlebars. Seat bags range in size from tiny to quite large and are made in a variety of styles and materials. Many riders like to spread their cargo among several smaller bags rather than keep it concentrated in panniers or one backpack. This strategy has been used with great success by ultra-endurance mountain bike racers.

Around the world, everyday bicyclists carry whatever they need in low-tech baskets, most often attached to the front of the bike. These are extremely convenient, but putting cargo in the front has a small effect on the ability to navigate tricky obstacles at low speed. Using an open basket also means that whatever's in there will go flying out in the event of a minor crash.

Small seat bags can hold a few important tools, maybe some keys and change, and not much else.

PRO TIP: If you are frequently hauling a laptop computer, think about using a machine with a solid-state hard drive. Even if you never crash, the constant jostling of riding the streets can ruin a regular hard drive. Carrying the machine in a backpack or messenger bag is the best way to buffer road vibration.

WHAT TO WEAR?

Beware of the old wives who say you must wear certain bike-specific clothes to cycle-commute. In fair weather you can commute in pretty much whatever clothing you'd like. You can wear the old standby shorts and a T-shirt and a pair of sneakers. Maybe you just commute in your work clothes. Lots of folks pull this off, even some who work in business suits. So lots of different clothes can work, even jeans. On the other hand, certain items of bicycling clothing can be beneficial, even in nice weather.

Sunglasses provide protection from the sun and also from flying objects, such as bugs or pebbles thrown up by the front tire.

We've already discussed bike shoes a bit, but that's the tip of the iceberg. It's hard to beat the comfort of riding in chamois-crotched Lycra shorts and a lightweight jersey. Light and skin-hugging, it's kind of like riding in high-tech underwear. Bike jerseys and jackets usually have useful pockets in back. Cycling gloves definitely add some comfort, block the sun, and protect your hands in case of minor falls. There's nothing particularly special about cycling socks. The amount of protection that bicycle helmets actually provide is a murky and controversial subject (the helmet makers are careful to point out that their product is designed to protect in the event of minor, toppling-over type falls, not collisions with motor vehicles), but the helmets are undeniably comfortable and cool. When shopping for a new helmet, keep in mind that the cheap ones protect just as well as the expensive ones.

WINTER GEAR

Cold, wet commutes are another matter entirely. In terrible weather, good clothes are more important than simple comfort. A waterproof, windproof shell is important. A waterproof, windproof, and *breathable* shell is amazingly useful (and expensive). Try to find one with bright reflective strips. Beneath the jacket, you can use many different types of insulating garments on the upper half of the body, from a fleece pullover to a long-sleeved wool jersey to a plain old wool sweater. Against the skin, wear a layer composed of something that wicks moisture and helps keep the skin dry (e.g., wool or polypropylene). This is important for the winter bicyclist, who will often generate enough inner heat to cause an outbreak of sweating, even on very cold days. There's an art to layering just right to balance the outer cold and the intense warmth the body generates with exercise, and this balance will be different for each individual.

If cold, wet weather was the only problem associated with winter commuting, commuters would have it made.

On the bottom half, the rider can use a number of different strategies. There are bike-specific tights, some of cozy wool, and weatherproof cycling pants. For the head, wear a Lycra skullcap or balaclava beneath a helmet.

Commuters who like to wear racy bike shoes have trouble with that arrangement when it's cold and wet, turning to various types of shoe covers. Even with shoe covers, their feet often turn into numb blocks. Another tactic for the feet is to start with a more substantial type of shoe that provides better protection from the elements. Some riders like to use a cheaper, lunkier bike shoe, a half-size too large and stuffed with two pairs of thick wool socks. Others go whole hog and opt to ride in waterproof winter boots, which can be used with platform pedals or large toe clips.

Fact is, you can beat just about any type of weather with the right clothing. But winter riding comes with an even greater challenge for the bicyclist—icy streets. (See "Reading the Road Surface," p. 45.)

RIDING IN YOUR WORK CLOTHES

What you wear during the commute has something to do with the situation at your destination. Will you be able to shower, or even to change? Will you need to?

Ideally you could commute in your work clothes and make a seamless transition from bike to work without having to worry about looking like a complete disaster. Lots of folks pull this off, but it's problematic. Here are three common ways that bike commuting will mess with your clothing:

Drivetrain contamination. The bicycle chain drive is the evil archenemy of clean pants. A serious, dedicated commuting bike might have a chain case or cover to protect pants (or long 1800s-style skirts). If you don't have a chain case and still want to save your pants, roll them up pretty far—and then a little more. This helps ensure that any black chain glorp that gets on the

Riding in office clothes can be surprisingly comfortable. However, there are many ways that commuting can ruin clothing for almost any other use.

pant leg will soil only the inside of the garment. The pant leg can also be secured around the ankle with a piece of Velcro webbing, available at your local bike shop; most of these also feature helpful reflective strips.

Seat stain. Dealing with the pant leg is just the opening battle however. In the rain or, not to put too fine a point on it, in the sweat, the black hue of the typical bike seat will be transferred to whatever clothing stands between the seat and your bum. For this reason, avoid riding in light-colored trousers or shorts.

Back splatter. Ride through a single murky puddle, and you'll be rewarded with a streak of brown droplet stains, right up your backside. It's not water that we're talking about here. It's the oil and grime of the street, and once it gets all over your clothing, it's probably not coming out. A good set of fenders will take care of this problem.

The longer the commute, the more difficult it will be to ride in office clothes. Even if you keep the clothes clean, it can be difficult to keep them from getting soaked with sweat. Most long-distance commuters ride to work in one set of clothes, then change into their work clothes. This implies a double challenge: They not only have to find some place to stash "used" bike clothes at the workplace but must also figure out a passable way to bring the work clothes with them on the bike—a mind-bender due to the wrinkle factor alone—or keep them at work.

Those who drive to work some days can use those days to haul clothing back and forth. "I keep up to three pairs of shoes at work," says Shawn. "You don't want to be stuck wearing bike shoes at work, and that's the one item I tend to forget. Plus, shoes can be heavy." Those who carry clothing back and forth on the bike can mitigate wrinkling by using fabrics that are less wrinkle-prone. Panniers are available that double as garment bags and keep your clothes looking sharp. There are also products designed especially for transporting clothes with minimal wrinkling.

This logistical challenge is unique to the bicycle commuter. Neither car commuters nor recreational bicyclists have to think about these things.

PART II:
Preparation

ROUTE CHOICE AND PLANNING

So you've equipped yourself so outrageously with the latest, greatest gear that a coalition of bike shop owners has lobbied to create a new national holiday named for your first-born son. But are you ready to hit the street? Nope. Not until you work out a plan for your route to work. Route choice is one of the most powerful tools at the cycle-commuter's disposal, but it's often underappreciated or neglected by beginners.

First of all, it's important to realize that your favored route to get to work in the car could be absolutely nasty on a bike. Many beginners just copy the same route they've been driving,

A simple shortcut like this bridge for pedestrians and bicyclists could shave a lot of time off your commute. Be creative, and let the advantages of travel by bike work for you.

An unmapped tunnel beneath a highway gives local bicyclists and pedestrians an important commuter route.

with predictably unpleasant results. Bike commuters should get much more creative in route planning.

Except for some freeways, bridges, and tunnels, bicyclists are allowed to operate their vehicles on almost all public streets, with the same rights and responsibilities as drivers of cars and trucks. So expect to chart an interesting bicycle-specific route to your destination, using relatively bike-friendly roads wherever possible.

Remember that bicyclists also have the freedom to use many non-street thoroughfares, including multiuse paths and even sidewalks in some cases. These facilities can sometimes be used to cut a more direct path through a city, or at least provide little shortcuts. When your route is perfected, it's likely to contain at least a few interesting non-street elements.

Initial planning of your route could be as simple as looking at a good map. (Beware of maps that are simplified by omitting many minor streets. Serious commuters need serious maps.) Most cities produce a bicycle map that shows official bike routes: bike paths and streets purported to be bike-friendly. Some streets that have been labeled bike routes have bike lanes painted on them. Not all bike-laned streets are created equal, however, although they may appear that way on a map. Other official bike routes have "sharrows," stencils on the road surface with a bicycle symbol and an arrow, which are intended to send a message to both cyclists and drivers. Some official bike routes don't have either of these features but have been deemed wide enough or otherwise conducive to safe and pleasant riding.

Streets that go *through*—crossing highways or waterways—will be the key streets getting you where you need to go. These are the streets you will *need* to use, if only briefly, whether or not they are classified as bike routes. Unfortunately, these may also be very unfriendly to cyclists. In extreme cases, use only the block or two of the street that you need. Even on these short stretches, it may be possible to use a sidewalk if the street is truly heinous. The rest of your route will be up to you and can be changed at will on a daily basis.

Sharrows —shared-use arrows—are meant to send a message to both drivers and cyclists. They are thought to calm traffic and alert motorists to the presence of cyclists, while encouraging cyclists to ride on the correct side of the street. Some advocates feel that sharrows offer all the advantages of bike lanes without the disadvantages, but others find them completely ineffective.

THE GOOD, THE BAD, AND THE ANNOYING

Lack of route choice is an undeniable problem for many commuters in some nonurban areas, who are locked on busy, high-speed back roads. They would gladly use some deserted residential street if available but continue commuting on the route they're given, proving that you don't need an ideal route to commute successfully.

What would the ideal route look like anyway? To some it's as simple as finding the most direct or least hilly route. Point and shoot. Others go out of their way to find extra hills and extra miles! Literally, bike commuters are all over the map when it comes to route preferences. There are as many "ideal" routes as there are individual commuters. Certainly, however, bike commuters have some preferences, and annoyances, in common.

It's interesting how two completely different types of streets can both be considered bike-friendly. Most riders prefer to travel on streets with relatively few motor vehicles. Quiet streets that are comfortably wide are often considered bike-friendly. The term may also be applied to a busy and narrow downtown street where bicyclists easily travel at the same speed as motor traffic.

Planning officials have their own ideas about what makes a bike-friendly street. Most cities have networks of marked bike routes.

Cyclists often feel comfortable riding on either of these road types, but they are about as different as can be.

Perhaps the most important ingredient of a bike-friendly street is the attitude of the people who use it. Where a large percentage of road users expect bicyclists and go out of their way to accommodate them, the commute is noticeably easier. Unfortunately, such places are not exactly common.

Any number of factors start to chip away at bike-friendliness. One of the most important is on-street parking, which negatively affects the cyclist's line of sight to potential hazards coming from the side and forces the rider farther left to avoid potential "doorings"—collisions with car doors.

Of course you probably won't be able to avoid streets with side parking, or any of the other negative features that affect commuters' happiness and safety, for very long. The venue we've been given is not ideal; it's crowded with obstacles and trouble spots. But with a little creative route choice, we can make the most of it.

What in particular makes a bad route?

- **High traffic speeds.** High speeds decrease comfort level for cycling while increasing injuries in case of collision. High-speed two-lane highways can be particularly stressful when traffic is heavy. Remember that high speed limits don't benefit bicyclists, who rarely move faster than 30 miles per hour on the flats.

- **On-street parking** decreases visibility, spawns frequent conflicts, and, because of the need to stay out of the "Door Zone" [see "The Door Zone," p. 50], decreases the usable width of the roadway. Unfortunately, on-street parking is so common in urban areas that it is difficult if not impossible to avoid.

- **Time-sapping traffic signals.** Foot down, sucking exhaust. It's one of the least glamorous aspects of the bike commute. Sitting at red lights also consumes a lot more time than is generally realized.

- **Wandering pedestrians.** It's hard to keep track of them all, but you must do your best or risk getting taken out. It's best just to avoid areas with swarms of people on foot, if possible.

- **Entrances and exits to shopping centers and other attractions.** These are an indication that drivers will be attempting to turn across your line frequently, which greatly increases the chances for mishap.

- **Freeway entrance and exit ramps.** These combine high speeds with impatient, head-swiveling motorists.

- **High schools.** At certain times of day, the streets around American high schools are occupied with some of the least experienced, most aggressive drivers imaginable. Grade schools and middle schools, with their parades of motoring parents, are sources of great frustration for bike commuters as well.

- **Choppy street surfaces and heavy road damage** are common annoyances.

- **Broken glass, thorns or other sources of punctures.** If you keep getting flats on your route, it's worth changing.

- **Bad attitudes.** You'll find the microculture of some streets and areas of town noticeably more hostile than others.

These problems may not be apparent right away, revealing themselves slowly and annoyingly over time. Adjust the route accordingly. Route choice is a process, not a one-time event.

Ideally, the route-finding process will leave you with a route that is actually—get this—fun. At that point you're getting to and from work safely while improving your health, and having a great time doing it.

INTERMODAL

When considering a commute, don't give up if you decide the trip is too long for bicycling.

More and more cycle-commuters are getting to work by combining a bike commute with travel by some other mode—car, bus, train, or boat. This is extremely useful when the trip is long, and it could potentially save a lot of time if the transition is smooth. Likewise, if some particularly nasty portion of the route is keeping you in the car, it might be possible to drive through that part and ride the rest.

The realities of intermodal travel introduce a new set of complications and considerations. Bike choice, for instance, might change depending on the intermodal situation in question. If you have to put the bike in a rack on the front of a city bus, you might opt for a junker; if you have to carry it on a train, you might choose a folding bike or lean toward a machine that is extra light and easy to handle. Intermodal travel also implies more reliance on others, so time savings could get consumed by various situations out of your control.

DRESS REHEARSAL

Experienced commuters have some further advice on this subject: Pre-ride the route! Don't go out and try an unknown route for the first time on a workday, unless it's an extremely simple route and you're already very familiar with the areas in question. Route-related puzzles and surprises have a way of asserting themselves on a first attempt through unknown neighborhoods. Work out all the confusion ahead of time, not amid the stress of an actual commute.

PRE-RIDE INSPECTION

It's a good idea to give your bike a quick once-over before heading out for any sort of ride. This is especially true for commutes, which are usually very time-sensitive operations. You can't afford to sit by the side of the road fiddling with your bike all morning. Almost like time-trialists in the Tour de France (sure, why not), commuters rely on consistent, if not flawless, operation of their machines. But you don't enjoy the services of a live-in mechanic to tune and inspect your bike. Am I being overly dramatic, or not dramatic enough? Getting to work on time can be very serious business.

- **Tire pressure.** Give it the old thumb test. Better yet, throw a floor pump with pressure gauge on there, and make sure it shows at least the minimum pressure recommended for that specific tire. Often you'll find that one or both tires are slowly but steadily losing air. These slow leaks can be tricky. They can go quite a while without being detected but may eventually cause a wreck when the half-flat state of the tire is exposed in a hard turn. Some riders like to fix every little leak as they find it; others opt to repump briefly every morning until it becomes absolutely necessary to repair or replace the tube.

- **Spin the wheels.** This allows you to see anomalies in the rim or tire. Pay special attention to weird bulges in the tire itself. The tire may be close to failing or may not be properly attached to the rim, which is equally dangerous. Are the brakes rubbing? Adjust accordingly.

- **Make sure the front wheel is securely attached to the front fork.** A lot of beginners get this wrong, leaving their quick-release open or loose. Might as well check the rear wheel too, although it's the front that could kill you.

- **Apply the brakes.** Make sure they work smoothly and easily stop the wheels. Time for new pads?

- **Quickly check the handlebars, stem, headset, etc., to make sure they remain tight.** No play or rattles. But resist any temptation to overtighten. Seat creaking? Some bolts may need a little tightening. Address creaks in the front end quickly. If they aren't solved by tightening the handlebars or headset, or by lubing cables, the bike might have a cracked bar, stem, steer tube, or frame.

- **Does the chain need lubrication?** Probably. Were the derailleur pulleys making that awful squeak on the ride home last night? Lube for success. Wipe the excess. Do not ingest.

- **Test your lights.** Make sure they function and are charged or have good batteries.

PART III:
The Ride

HANDLING THE MACHINE

While most beginners are focused on the harrowing prospect of being hit by a car, the truth is that bicyclists are injured much more often in solo wipeouts than in collisions. Of course the car-bike collisions tend to cause more severe injuries and are responsible for most of the fatalities—and spark all the headlines—but bicyclists don't need collisions or cars to injure themselves. According to the US Consumer Product Safety Commission's National Electronic Injury Surveillance System, only about 15 percent of bicyclists who get banged up badly enough to visit an emergency room are victims of car-bike collisions. So before we get into traffic cycling and all that juicy stuff, let's begin at the beginning: staying upright. This will be your most persistent concern as a bicyclist.

Riding skill obviously comes into play here. In some corners of the bicycle universe, people like to pretend that it doesn't, or shouldn't. But handling a bicycle is something of an athletic endeavor. That's not to say you need to have catlike reflexes or the body of an Olympian to do it well. If you did possess these attributes, however, they could be quite useful.

Consider this small fact: Whereas drivers steer their vehicles through mechanical means using only small movements of the hands and feet, bicyclists steer with the entire body. Stopping the bike quickly also requires a coordinated full-body movement. Sitting heavily on the seat and yanking on a lever won't produce the desired results. The mechanism for turning and stopping the bicycle is . . . *you*. This is a fact of life, not an endorsement or condemnation of any particular style of riding. Not only is it a fact of life, it's something to be celebrated. The full-body, athletic act that is maneuvering a bicycle has its own reward—it's fun! Add another wheel, and you make a much more stable vehicle but seriously compromise the fun. Riding a bicycle through a turn is like floating, flying. Riding a tricycle through a turn is like wrestling a shopping cart full of canned beans.

RELAX!

Relaxation is the key to smooth bike handling. Release all the unnecessary tension in your muscles. Beginners tend to hold themselves very stiff on the bike. Imagine how this affects something as seemingly simple as balancing the machine, which depends on relatively tiny, instantaneous movements of the body and handlebars. Relaxed riders also make their own suspension on supple arms and legs—far better on the road than any mechanical shock absorber. And of course relaxed riders won't tire as quickly.

Riders with quick reflexes who are smooth and relaxed on the bike are less likely to crash than those who ride stiffly with sluggish reflexes. If they hit something or start to slide out, the quick, smooth, and relaxed riders are more likely to recover; if unable to recover, they are less likely to be injured.

Even stiff-as-a-board novices can learn smooth handling skills. If you're feeling sketchy, visit some semi-deserted expanse of pavement to engage in some old-fashioned trial and error. Train yourself to perform the basic moves. We're talking about turning and stopping, essentially. Be vigorous but not dangerously so. Swoop into some turns, and learn how to relax your body and look *through* the turn rather than down at the ground. Try some hard stops (sometimes called "panic stops"). Feel how your body has to lunge backward dramatically to keep the bike in control during very intense stops. Try some stops using each brake alone to feel the different requirements for weight distribution. If you feel yourself floating over the bike rather than sitting on the saddle like a sack of potatoes (the favored position of the beginning cyclist), you've already come a long way.

It's also important to practice riding in a straight line. In particular, learn not to swerve into traffic when turning your head around.

- - - - - - - - - - - - - - - - - -

PRO TIP: For a more advanced course, ride your bike—especially a skinny-tired road bike—on dirt. This will give you a feel for traction and body position on varied surfaces.

- - - - - - - - - - - - - - - - - -

READING THE ROAD SURFACE

Unlike drivers of cars, the bicyclist must pay special attention to road damage, cracks, gravel, and other seemingly benign features. A pothole that may be barely noticed inside a car might send the rider flying. For this reason (and for many others), bicycling requires a fundamentally different mind-set than driving a car.

If you're new to this, you'll have to start looking at your world with an eye for details that you previously ignored. Typically bicyclists learn which details are important the hard way. There's no more effective form of teaching than that—insta-pain—but it would be preferable to learn about these things ahead of time. If you haven't yet learned the hard way, be aware of the following:

- **Potholes.** Everyone hits potholes occasionally, and usually it's no big deal. However, a pothole may cause a wreck if the rider doesn't see it coming. A violent pothole strike could also cause some damage to the bicycle (or the rider's wrists), even if it doesn't cause a fall. Avoid potholes by looking far ahead and minutely adjusting your direction of travel. Should you find yourself on course for a pothole that can't be avoided, try to go over it if you can. Bunny-hop the hole or, at least, lift the front wheel over. Dealing with potholes, or any rough feature, demands that you lift your weight from the saddle and suspend your body on bent arms and legs. Then, even if you strike the edge of the pothole, you stand a chance of maintaining control.

- **Railroad tracks.** Tracks can cause quick, violent wrecks in a few different ways. They tend to stick up above street level, so they can catch the tire and divert it suddenly, throwing the rider down. Even if the tracks are flush with the street, however, the metal strips provide almost no traction. If an unsuspecting rider puts the front tire on a track that is at an angle to the bicyclist's direction of travel, or onto a perpendicular track while leaning the bike over or applying any sort of sideways force, the bike could be dumped to the ground with astounding speed. This danger is compounded greatly when the tracks are wet. Treat wet railroad tracks, and any other wet metal surfaces, as if they were made of ice. In fact, if they were made of ice, that would be something of an improvement.

- **Longitudinal cracks.** Longi—*what*? Longitudinal cracks are straight cracks or seams running parallel to the direction of travel. They may be caused by surface fatigue, although more likely they will be man-made. Joints between blocks of concrete are the most common form. If the front tire falls into one of these things, a crash isn't certain, but it's very likely. Balancing the bike depends on constant adjustments of the front wheel. In these crashes, the front tire is caught in the rut just long enough to upset the whole system.

- **Gravel.** Patches of gravel have rudely educated many bicyclists over the years. Sand, gravel, marbles, Tic-Tacs, BBs

Longitudinal cracks are often overlooked by beginners.

. . . if it's all over the street, don't try to turn your bike on it. Straighten the bike to vertical, and ride through patches of tiny friction-killing objects without using the brakes. Attempting to brake hard on gravel will put you right down on the gravel-covered tarmac.

— **Water.** Many solid surfaces become dangerously slick with the addition of a little water. When wet, concrete provides roughly half as much friction for your tires as it does when dry. Pay special attention to the white lines on the street too—they're very slippery in the rain. Wet metal, as already mentioned, is as slippery as glare ice, or worse. Don't ride aggressively into puddles—there may be a wheel-catching grate or pothole hidden under the water.

— **Ice.** Ice is more likely than any other surface to cause a painful wreck. If you must ride on icy streets, use studded tires. These are commercially available or can be prepared at home. Even studded tires cannot fully neutralize the brutality of ice, however. An icy commute must be tackled in a slow, deliberate fashion. Expect the icy winter version of your commute to take much longer than the dry summer version.

Surface hazards are a fact of life. Even expert bicyclists hit the deck once in a while. These falls can result in injury, but often they are just unpleasant. Your likelihood of falling will be greatly decreased with experience. Perhaps another way to say that is: Your experience will be greatly increased with falls. Like much of bike safety, staying upright depends on a simple directive: *Watch where you're going.*

RIDE SMART

Bicyclists can eliminate a lot of problems with other roadway users simply by riding conservatively, considerately, and deliberately, according to basic traffic rules. In particular, cyclists should ride *with* traffic, on the right side of the road. Riding against traffic is a common cause of collisions, in addition to being against the law.

Think about exactly *why* riding "contraflow" leads to collisions. When a cyclist is moving against traffic—on the sidewalk or the road—drivers pulling out onto the parallel street will be looking left for traffic as the cyclist approaches from their right. One of the most egregious bonehead rookie mistakes is to roll in front of these drivers, who aren't even looking in your direction, while moving against traffic on the wrong side of the street.

Simply following the law will eliminate most of these situations, but not all of them. In some instances you may find yourself riding against traffic legally on a side path or in a two-way bike lane. Legal or not, the same basic principles apply.

RIDE DEFENSIVELY

Cyclists looking for advice about cycling in traffic tend to get a very dry response from official sources and bicycling safety literature. The response usually amounts to: "Follow the law. Ride predictably, and follow the law. Oh, and wear your helmet." But is that enough? Unfortunately, it's not nearly enough.

Looking through piles of statistics from decades of car-bike collisions, we can see that riding in a lawful fashion is not great protection against getting hit by a car. Certainly many wrecks can be blamed on the indiscretions of bicyclists, but according to recent studies, in the majority of car-bike collisions involving *adult* bicyclists, the driver overlooked and collided with a bicyclist who was riding lawfully. Most of these crashes are caused by what is known as the "looked-but-failed-to-see error"—the driver turns into or pulls out in front of a bicyclist that he or she failed to notice. The cyclist's vulnerability to being overlooked by well-meaning drivers is probably the single most important thing to understand about riding a bike in traffic.

Considering the particular challenges facing bicyclists, a *defensive* approach is the best approach. Keep your head up, eyes forward, and be on constant lookout for motorist mistakes. Maintain an attitude of readiness. If you have to, make a game out of it. As one very experienced rider puts it, "I imagine that there is not one driver out there who is actually paying attention." Thankfully, a vigilant rider can avoid most types of collisions. Ride *ready,* and you'll be as safe as you can be.

This is really just common defensive driving strategy applied to bicycling.

THE MOST COMMON MOTORIST MISTAKES THAT LEAD TO CAR-BIKE CRASHES

Left turn into cyclist. These are some of the most consistently damaging wrecks suffered by cyclists. The angle tends to be nearly head-on, and speeds can be deadly fast. Keep in mind that many drivers don't even slow down before cranking the turn. Be aware not only of oncoming traffic but also of any streets or driveways on the right onto which left turns might occur. What I call the "Gap Effect" comes into play during the so-called "left cross" collision: Impatient motorists see a gap in oncoming traffic, have their eyes set on oncoming cars, and fail to notice the bicyclist in the gap.

Pullout from a stop sign. Quick glances from motorists don't do the trick, and they pull right out into the path of another road user. Very common—be ready for it.

Right hook. The right hook is another common motorist error. Motorists pass a cyclist and immediately attempt a right turn into the space occupied by the cyclist. This results from poor judgment as well as looked-but-failed-to-see problems. Bicyclists also cause their own right hooks by attempting to pass vehicles on the right at the wrong time. Cyclists can avoid right hooks easily with a little forethought and creative positioning.

THE DOOR ZONE

Special hazards exist on streets with parallel parking. Bicyclists on these streets must be on the lookout for vehicles entering or exiting parking spaces, and for pedestrians darting out into the road from between vehicles. The space within about 4 feet of

Not all bike lanes are created equal. The bike lane in the photo lies almost entirely within the door zone of the parked vehicles, creating a dangerous situation for unsuspecting cyclists.

the parked vehicles is a bit like a minefield for cyclists. Bicyclists riding here are vulnerable to having a car door thrown open suddenly in front of them. Doorings are a regretfully common and painful experience for novice cyclists, but there is an easy cure: Don't ride in the Door Zone. Avoid riding on streets where avoiding the Door Zone becomes problematic.

With a little bit of confidence, riders begin to think they can see into passenger compartments with enough acuity to predict when a door will pop open. Unfortunately they are usually incorrect, but it takes yet another layer of experience to realize it. Again: Don't ride in the Door Zone.

USING MULTIUSE PATHS AND SIDEWALKS

The supremacy of the bicycle lies partly in its ability to prowl both the vehicular and pedestrian realms. This special power is at once underappreciated and badly abused. When riding in the pedestrians' realm, remember that they always have the right-of-way, even on sidewalks and paths that are open to bikes, and be especially courteous to people on foot.

Denver commuters are lucky to have well-designed, fully separated paths available. Negotiating the path around lots of other users, however, can be a challenge.

Don't assume that you'll always be faster using streets and riding with motor vehicles. Very well-built facilities might be available that flow under streets and intersections and act like mini freeways for bikes. Without stop signs or traffic lights, these actually provide faster travel than surface streets. Some communities are very well equipped with these separate paths, having installed them next to almost every suitable waterway and highway, while most American cities go without.

Use of bike paths can be deceivingly tricky. Beginners are drawn to these facilities because they seem safer, less hectic. When so many beginners are on the path at the same time, however, combined with the pedestrians, joggers, dogs, pigeons, and what-have-you, negotiating these facilities is probably more likely to result in some kind of crack-up than riding on the street. Side paths that cross streets are the trickiest facilities of all, with a high rate of turning- and crossing-related collisions. This was revealed most dramatically in a recent study of car-bike collisions performed by the City of Boulder's Transportation Department. About half the car-bike crashes reported in the study occurred when the bicyclist was crossing a street from a sidewalk or side path.

As always, it's difficult to determine what's to blame: the facility type or the riders who are drawn to it. It's probably a combination of both. Experienced riders understand that the danger of a street, path, or intersection is largely determined by individual riders—what they know and how they apply it. Good riders can deal with bad facilities, just like they deal with bad drivers. At the same time, some facility designs do promote or mitigate certain types of conflicts. For instance, contraflow side paths will lead to an elevated number of collisions with right-turning vehicles, and bike lanes that are entirely outside Door Zones will minimize doorings.

Using sidewalks is not always illegal and, depending on the rider's personal preferences and style, may be useful occasionally. But riding on sidewalks often requires more awareness and handling prowess than riding in the street. So if you're turning

As this sign indicates, bike paths beside waterways are prone to flooding.

to sidewalks as an escape from street traffic, it might be a frying pan–to-fire situation.

Sidewalk riders not only have to defer to pedestrians' right-of-way at all times but also have to respect their "flinch zones," for lack of a better term. This means leaving a wide buffer when passing pedestrians and always passing at near-walking speed. Try to allow walkers to move as they would if you weren't there. (That advice might be complicated by the fact that there is often a legal requirement to give some audible signal before passing a pedestrian.)

But pedestrian relations are just one part of it. Anyplace where sidewalks meet streets and alleys—and they always do—disasters await the too-casual or inexperienced sidewalk bicyclist. So, yes, use the occasional sidewalk in your commute if it expedites your travels or somehow makes life easier, but make sure you understand the special requirements and necessary skills first.

RUSH HOUR

If only we could choose the time of our commute as well as the route. Few of us have that luxury. If we did, we'd choose to ride sometime other than rush hour.

Rush hour traffic has peculiar properties. First of all, of course, there are a lot more cars on the road, a lot more pedestrians, a lot more encounters and potential collisions. But the traffic itself is different. While city traffic typically consists of a high percentage of professional drivers, during rush hour the streets are flooded with amateurs. They are less experienced and less aware than professional drivers. In addition, they tend to be even more anxious and distracted during rush hours. In the morning they may be running late and freaking out, or they may be "multitasking," attempting to apply makeup or shave instead of watching the road. At night they just want to get home as fast as possible.

So cycle-commuters get to deal with greater numbers of dangerous drivers, at times when they are acting more dangerous than usual.

For bicycling facilities like fully separated paths, rush hour might be a very different beast. Bike paths are more useful for speedy transportation during rush hours on weekdays than they tend to be on weekends, when the recreational wanderers come out.

RIDING IN THE DARK

There are a few things that really stand out in bicycling accident statistics. One of the most glaring is the portion of fatal collisions that occur during non-daylight hours. According to the Insurance Institute for Highway Safety (IIHS), almost half the cyclist fatalities in 2010 occurred between the hours of 6 p.m. and 6 a.m. (The full report is available at www.iihs.org/research/fatality.aspx?topicName=Bicycles&year=2010.) Consider the relatively few cyclists on the streets during these hours. This unusual deadliness is due to poor visibility, of course, but also the prevalence of drunk vehicle operators. A strikingly large percentage of nighttime fatalities involve intoxicated drivers, intoxicated bicyclists, or both. IIHS reports that the percentage of all cyclist fatalities involving a drunk vehicle operator usually hovers between 25 and 30 percent, but at night this percentage would go significantly higher.

When we add good lighting and sober cycling to the mix, night riding isn't nearly as dangerous, but it's still not great. If you have the choice, ride during daylight. Even better, ride when the sun is slightly higher in the sky and not flaming directly into drivers' eyes.

But don't get scared away from bike commuting just because you have to ride in the dark. Just be aware of the extra challenge. Adjust your route to minimize reliance on the eyes of strangers driving at high speed, move in a very deliberate fashion, and light yourself up like a Donald Trump high-rise. (See "Lights," page 20.)

PREDICTING PEDESTRIAN BEHAVIOR

If you observe pedestrians long enough, you'll notice some disturbing patterns. Pedestrians will often step out into the street from the curb or their recently parked vehicle without so much as a glance. Why? Their ears don't register the sound of an approaching motor vehicle, so their brain tells them the coast is clear. It's crazy, but true. Are we humans too lazy to turn our heads? Or are we just overconfident in our sense of hearing? Of course the bicyclist is relatively silent, and this leads to sudden, uncomfortable confrontations, and frequent bike-pedestrian smash-ups.

Pedestrians are also prone to the same sort of looked-but-failed-to-see errors exhibited by drivers. Street-crossers at inter-sections are some of the least aware of all road users, even when crossing against the light. They glance up meekly, if at all, fail to notice, and then point their eyes straight down at the pavement and start trudging across. If other pedestrians are making the same crossing, the lemming effect kicks in.

Experienced urban commuters keep their eagle eye on pedestrians as much as drivers and adjust their position proactively to avoid the classic pedestrian no-look run-out.

RIDING WITH HEADPHONES

To much of the public, riding a bike while listening to an iPod seems terribly dangerous. At the same time, driving a car with a soundproof passenger compartment with the stereo cranked up is rarely questioned. A bit inconsistent? Certainly. Yet laws have been passed in various cities and states prohibiting cyclists from using earbuds or, if you're old school like me, headphones while on a bicycle. Meanwhile, riding with headphones is more popular lately than it's been since the introduction of the Sony Walkman in the early 1980s.

My personal belief is that bicyclists can learn to ride in traffic without hearing the noise of traffic at all. For instance, deaf people can learn to ride in reasonable safety. It's also true that downtown traffic is often very loud to begin with—so loud that hearing the subtleties of traffic noise is often virtually impossible. We all know that drivers try to shut out the noise, and succeed, and still manage to drive through town. However, I think keeping your ears open to what's going on around you, especially behind you, makes life on the street a lot easier.

Depending on what you're listening to on your little electronic device and how loud you're listening to it, traffic noises might just come through loud and clear anyway. Listening to spoken word is not the same as listening to music. Loud music over headphones will drown out other sounds; a podcast or newscast will not. However, listening to someone talk, and trying to understand what he or she is saying, may be more *distracting*. Distractions are much more dangerous than decibels.

In my opinion, the better you are at cycling in traffic, the more unlikely it becomes that you will be able to comprehend a podcast while doing so. The state of awareness and vigilance necessary for riding safely in heavy traffic leaves little room for extraneous information. If you find that you have no problem understanding podcasts or having phone conversations while riding in the city, it could be a sign that you're doing it wrong.

WHAT DOES THE LAW *REALLY* SAY?

It's all well and good to say that bicyclists should follow traffic laws, but what exactly is in those laws? Maybe not what you think.

Traffic laws are set at local and state levels. They are different for each community but tend to conform to a general, traditional framework known as the Uniform Traffic Code. In many respects the law treats the bicycle like any other vehicle: Bicyclists must ride on the right side of the road, with traffic, and obey all speed limits, traffic control devices, and other directives. However, bicyclists are treated quite differently in some areas of the law. For example, bicyclists may be able to legally access some sidewalks and paths where motor vehicles are forbidden. On the other hand, bikes could be banned from using some freeways and other roadways.

Cyclists are also treated differently than other relatively slow-moving vehicles. Unlike a piece of slow-moving farm equipment, a bicyclist is not automatically allowed to "take the lane" in front of cars. Bicyclists are required to move to the right side of the road when faster traffic approaches to facilitate passing, unless there are potholes or parked cars on the side, the lane is too narrow for safe passing, or a similar situation. The law in most places is carefully written to leave it up to the cyclist's reasonable discretion whether it is safe to move right. But it is also carefully written to ensure that the final say on reasonableness of the cyclist's movements belongs to judges and juries, who are unlikely to fully understand the bicyclist's viewpoint. The rules on riding to the right have spawned a great deal of confusion.

Generally speaking, cyclists must move right for faster traffic unless:

- There is road damage or debris on the right side of the road.

- The cyclist is passing parked cars or slower bicyclists.

- The cyclist is moving at the same speed, or faster, as adjacent motor traffic.

- The cyclist intends to make a left turn or continue straight through an intersection with a right-turn-only lane.

- The lane (not including Door Zone or gutter) is too narrow for a motor vehicle to pass the cyclist safely within the lane.

It's the last of these that causes most of the confusion and is ultimately adjudicated on society's version of reasonableness. Different opinions about what exactly constitutes "safely" have led to more specifically worded ordinances governing motorists' passing of cyclists.

In the end, bicyclists need to act with common sense in their own self-interest, on a case-by-case basis, and nitpicking semi-memorized vagaries of local law while doing so is not going to be helpful.

While we're on the subject, don't forget to throw in a little cooperation and consideration for your fellow human beings. Don't fall into the trap of us-versus-them thinking while on your bike. We're all in this together. Look for opportunities to be courteous and helpful to others; it will make everybody's travels, including yours, a little bit easier.

LOCAL PECULIARITIES IN THE LAW

Check the local ordinances to find out what, if any, weirdness has been applied to you and your commute. What's legal in one city may be strictly *verboten* in another.

In some cities bicyclists are required to use a side path (a multiuse path paralleling a road—essentially a glorified side-walk) if one is provided. Riding on sidewalks, on the other hand, is usually illegal, but ordinances vary. Some bike-happy cities like Seattle and Madison, Wisconsin, are much more lenient about sidewalk riding, allowing it under certain conditions.

In many places, including Denver, a bicyclist is explicitly required to be inside the bike lane if one exists whenever there is faster traffic approaching, unless the rider is planning on turning left. Portland, Oregon, tried something different by giving bicy-clists within bike lanes blanket right-of-way over right-turning vehicles. Some cycling advocates find this law controversial, however, because it legitimizes cyclist movements that are con-trary to the normal vehicular dance, in which right-turning vehi-cles are to the right of straight-through vehicles.

Cycling advocacy in Madison also took a strange turn on the way to becoming law. In Madison it's *illegal* for a bicyclist

In some cities it's legal to ride on the left side of one-way streets.

to ride in the Door Zone. The idea behind this is to remove any ambiguity about the cyclist's proper place on the road and thus decrease cyclists' injuries. In most cities, riding within the Door Zone is considered lawful behavior, and the legal burden is placed on the driver to make sure the coast is clear before opening a door, but perhaps this leads to more doorings. (Doorings do not appear to be a significant source of crashes in Madison, although it's difficult to tell from their annual crash report.) Madison's Door Zone law would be incompatible with the bike lane law of Denver, where many bike lanes inhabit the Door Zone.

NEW LAWS TO PROTECT CYCLISTS

Colorado, Chicago, and several other places have passed laws that toughen penalties for drivers whose mistakes injure "vulnerable road users," typically defined as motorcyclists, pedestrians, and bicyclists. (These laws came about partly as a result of a strong alliance between motorcyclists and bicyclists.) In similar spirit, many local and state codes have adopted or will soon adopt some version of the "Three Foot Law," which requires motorists to leave at least 3 feet of space when passing a bicyclist. Versions of this well-meaning legislation have been put into effect in at least twenty-two states so far; Pennsylvania has a 4-foot passing law.

Bicyclists put a lot of energy into getting these safe passing laws on the books, but their actual effectiveness is debatable. For instance, a 2011 Johns Hopkins study found that Maryland's new 3-foot law was being widely ignored by motorists in Baltimore. Even if motorists do follow the law, a 3- or 4-foot pass still has the potential to be quite scary, depending on the vehicle and its speed.

Safe passing laws should at least be helpful in clarifying legal fault after the fact in the event of hit-from-behind collisions. If you hit somebody, you obviously didn't leave 3 feet of space! However, after a 3-foot law was signed in New York, cycling advocates there were dismayed to find that drivers who fatally struck bicyclists from behind continued to get sent home without so much as a traffic ticket. Furthermore, these laws tend to set shockingly low fines and penalties for injuring bicyclists, leaving many to wonder if we were better off before the laws were passed. Did we really need new laws? Or is it really new attitudes about cycling that we need? In a just world, drivers involved in hit-from-behind collisions would receive automatic *careless driving* citations for clear violations of basic vehicular laws already on the books.

Some states have also passed antiharassment laws to protect cyclists from excessive honking, yelling, and throwing of items by angry motorists—not necessarily a good sign.

AGAINST THE LAW

Talk about variations in the law. In Idaho bicyclists are allowed to treat stop signs like yield signs and treat red lights like stop signs. By all accounts, this seemingly radical departure from traditional traffic law works just fine. There has been no significant increase in collisions or dangerous behavior since the "stop-as-yield" law passed in 1982, and the job of the police has been made a bit easier. (The percentage of all reported crashes in Idaho involving a bicyclist is under 1 percent. Idaho cyclists were given further freedoms to take liberties with traffic lights in 2005.) Note that this law doesn't legalize reckless behavior by bicyclists. In fact, those who violate the rights-of-way of other users or act recklessly are probably more likely to be caught and cited in Idaho than elsewhere.

You may have noticed that a large percentage of riders, few of whom live in Idaho, already ride in this stop-as-yield mode. Clearly, many bicycle commuters are comfortable treating traffic lights like stop signs and stop signs like yield signs and can do so in reasonable safety. If they couldn't, the statistics would be quite different. There would be a huge increase in crashes to match the volume of law-stretching. Even with the blatant law-breaking that does occur, most collisions involving adult bicyclists are the result of their being overlooked by a motorist while riding lawfully. This is true even when including all the drunk and unlit night-riding crash victims.

Since police tend not to get overly excited about the benign lawbreaking of bicyclists, the door is left open for bicyclists to take more freedom than the written laws allow, and most do. While the law-breaking has not led to an epidemic of collisions, it has caused widespread outcry from the public, including law-abiding cyclists. And police who watch bicyclists roll through lights and stop signs are (even) less likely to take any bicyclist's side after a collision. Bicyclists' law-breaking is overblown as a safety issue, but it remains a minor public relations nightmare for bicyclists and bicycle transportation.

You might say to yourself, *Bicyclists are damned if they follow the law and damned if they don't, so why not take liberties where possible?* Another view holds that bicyclists' legitimacy as road users depends on their complying with the rules governing road users. Bicyclists who can be clipped, rammed, and dumped at any time by impatient motorists depend on this legitimacy. They should nurture and respect the law because its strength, in many ways, protects them. It's not only absurd but dangerous to selectively ignore those portions of the law we dislike while repeating chapter and verse those portions we can't live without. Many riders will argue this latter view—and then find themselves unable to resist nipping a red light for the sake of sheer convenience.

As it is, American cycle commuters are having their proverbial cake and eating it too. They depend on the law at the same time that they break it. While it could certainly be argued that motorists (and pedestrians) are doing the same thing, law-breaking bicyclists are more visible and widely resented.

To put it mildly, American cyclists have an interesting relationship with the law.

PART IV
At Work

HOW TO LOCK A BIKE

Unlike other types of utility cycling, commuting usually requires leaving the bike locked outside all day. This gives criminal opportunists a lot of time to become attracted by the shiny object and think of ways to take it. Still, it's not advisable to lock your bike in an out-of-the-way spot where thieves can work with impunity. It's better to leave it in moderately well-trafficked areas, in plain sight but not in the way. In this regard, the "secure" bike parking found in some buildings, often a fenced-off area in the parking garage, is a bit of a trade-off. Don't leave a valuable bicycle locked outside overnight, no matter how well it is secured.

Since your bike will be attached to it all day long, make sure that whatever you lock your bike to is itself secure. Some

Unfortunately, it's lock your bike or lose your bike.

Scars on the sidewalk are all that's left after an old, rusty bike rack was torn away in order to steal the bike that was locked to it.

dedicated bike racks are flimsy objects that weigh about as much as a lawn chair and aren't secured to the ground in any way. If you use a bike rack, make sure it's anchored firmly. Parking meters are just the right size and can work extremely well as makeshift bike racks, unless there are signs attached, which make it physically difficult to u-lock a bike to the meter. In New

York City and other places, locking a bike to a parking meter is illegal. A signpost could work in a pinch, provided of course that the post is firmly planted and there is a sign at the top to prevent someone from lifting your bike to freedom. An old thief trick is to prepare a "sucker post" that can be pulled from the ground if an unlucky individual locks a bike to it.

Your U-lock comes with two keys. Keep the spare in a secure location, and remember where you put it. If you use the same backpack or courier bag for each commute, keep the spare key tucked away in a special pocket. It's only a matter of time before you'll need it.

Thieves may ransack your bicycle even if it's locked up. Lights and cycle computers go missing. Seats and seatposts with quick-release clamping bolts (which started appearing on mountain bikes in the '80s) spawned a new cottage industry: tiny cable locks designed specifically to thwart theft of seats and seatposts.

Thieves often go after front wheels; rear wheels less often. Some commuters like to lock the front wheel or both wheels along with the frame. This can be done with a single U-lock by removing the front wheel. Some carry an extra cable lock to loop through both wheels. There are a couple schools of thought on this. It could be argued that locking the bike in this relatively extravagant fashion will make it more conspicuous and therefore a more likely target for thieves and vandals. Wheel theft can be thwarted with locking skewers instead of the typical thief-enabling quick-release variety, although these can make it more of a hassle to fix flats.

If someone wants your bike bad enough, you probably won't be able to stop the theft. So prevent the thief from wanting your bike in the first place. The shinier and prettier your bike is, the more desirable it will be. Consider the various ways you can "uglify" your bicycle without affecting its performance. For instance, you can remove the decals, paint the bike matte black, or, simplest of all, stop cleaning the frame. Before long it will be coated in beautiful, thief-repelling grunge. I used to receive a lot of comments and general grief about the impressive dirtiness of my Waterford road bike, but perhaps there was a method to my madness.

- -

PRO TIP: If you ride to the same rack every day, it may be possible to leave a U-lock locked on that rack so that you don't have to carry it. When you arrive, it will be waiting for you. If it's out in the weather, drop a little lube into the key hole once in a while. Possible pitfalls of this system: A maintenance guy might end up cutting the lock off if you don't have permission to leave it on a privately owned rack. Also, if it's your only lock, you're eventually going to need a lock for non-commuting purposes and won't have it with you. But if you've got an extra U-lock lying around, this is a great way to use it.

- -

WHAT TO DO WITH YOUR RIDING CLOTHES WHILE YOU'RE AT WORK

"I started laying my sweaty biking clothes out flat under my desk," says Giles. "They were totally hidden. I thought I had a great system. Then one day this crew comes in and starts intensively cleaning my workspace. They said, 'We've got some kind of mildew issue right around here, and we can't figure it out.' I didn't say anything."

If you're planning on riding to work in bike clothes and changing there, you may not have considered exactly how and where you're going to store your sweaty gear while you work. It's another problem unique to the bike commuter, and one for which there are no easy answers. Unfortunately, you can't just ball up the wet clothes and stash them in a backpack. Like Giles, you may opt to spread the clothes out somehow near your workspace. Jaime L. hangs her sweaty jersey and shorts in a bathroom stall, but she's not entirely comfortable with the arrangement and suspects some of her coworkers feel the same way. "I never really asked permission," she confesses. It may be possible to hang your "kit" on a windowsill, a fire escape, or in a seldom-used stairwell. If you are one of the lucky ones who can bring your commuting bike indoors, hang the clothes over the bike (unless they're dripping wet—sweat can corrode various parts of the bike).

THE WAR ON BODY ODOR

So you get to work *feeling* great but not *smelling* so great. If you have a shower at your disposal, fantastic. Consider yourself lucky. Most bike commuters have to make do without. Fear not, however. With a basic bathroom sink and some paper towels, you can clean yourself pretty well.

Some riders like to take it a step further and apply some kind of scent-masking device, such as deodorizers or essential oils of some sort.

By far the most common bit of advice offered by experienced bike commuters: baby wipes! When no shower is available, highly portable baby wipes allow for some degree of mopping up in critical bodily areas. Some veteran commuters swear by them. However, others are left unmoved by the power of the wipe. "It just leaves me feeling like sticky baby wipe," says Mary from Chicago. "Moist towelettes," like barbecue places give out, are similar to baby wipes but usually contain alcohol, which can dry the skin.

HELMET HAIR

"Some days it's horrible. Other days the helmet actually makes my hair look better!"

Ah, yes, the notorious helmet hair. It may be one of the most insidious and destructive forces working against the popularity of bicycling. I asked a very experienced commuter and helmet hair expert about her thoughts on the issue:

"Other than taking a shower and starting over, there's no truly effective way to fix a nasty mess of helmet hair after arriving at work. However, some methods can help a little. You can wet the hair a bit in the bathroom sink; if there is an electric hand dryer in the bathroom, use it to attack your helmet hair. Those hand dryers are the commuter's best friend." Unfortunately for sufferers of helmet hair, electric hand dryers seem to be going out of style with building managers.

Some commuters use powdered shampoo to deal with their sweaty, greasy helmet-shaped hair. I can't vouch for the effectiveness of this product, but there are those who swear by it.

THE "OTHER"

Bicycle commuters have to deal not only with traffic and weather and the logistics of riding but also with the reactions of a largely bicycling-averse society. These reactions range from admiration and envy, confusion and curiosity, to outright hatred and harassment. The bicyclist is, in many respects, the "other." The bicyclist is an object of conversation—often, whispered conversation. All bicyclists have to deal with these reactions from time to time, but commuting to work by bike adds another layer of complexity, as these reactions are coming from bosses, underlings, coworkers, and clients.

Most workplaces are populated largely by non-bicyclists, and commuting by bike tends to be quite the novelty. In this environment you have to expect that your bicycle commuting will become part of what defines you to others. If you're not careful, your mode of travel can *become* your workplace identity. You could very well become the "Bike Guy" or "Bike Lady." This happens far too often.

Your status as a bike commuter may affect, positively or negatively, how superiors and coworkers view your contribution.

People will make all kinds of assumptions about you based on your mode of travel alone. Many will assume that you are forced to travel by bike, although that is unlikely to be the case. Some may think you're riding due to environmentalist tendencies or that you're some kind of fitness fanatic. Some individuals who understand that you have made a conscious choice to ride a bike may believe that choice to be absolutely and literally insane. Who would ride a bike in that traffic? Biking to work might make people think you're strident, obsessed, or just plain crazy. No matter how far off base these impressions may be, it might be difficult to convince people otherwise.

The simple act of riding a bike for transportation is likely to leave a trail of blown minds and shattered perceptions at the workplace. This is the reality of bicycle commuting in North America. But the situation is changing for the better, largely due to people like you, who are out there showing everybody else how it's done.

PART V:
Routine Maintenance

PREVENTING PUNCTURES AND FLAT TIRES

Flat tires, or just the idea of them, keep a lot of would-be cyclists from chasing their two-wheeled dreams. And the prospect of flat tires while commuting is even more off-putting to the masses. It *is* a pain in the rear, no doubt about it. However, with a little bit of know-how and practice, you can slay the flat tire dragon.

Let's start with flat prevention. Beginning commuters tend to be so averse to the thought of having to fix or otherwise deal with a flat during a commute, they reach for all manner of specialized equipment in hopes of being able to forget about the issue. Favorite anti-flat equipment strategies include installing tires with extra-thick rubber or Kevlar belts, inserting plastic strips between the tire and the tube, and using tubes filled with a special ooze that are supposed to seal themselves when punctured. Some riders are so twisted up by the thought of the on-road puncture that they start to wonder about using solid rubber tires instead of pneumatics! All of these options come with significant drawbacks, to put it mildly. For instance, self-sealing "slime tubes," which don't always work, are not only extra heavy but impossible to patch because of the substance in the tube. In attempting to make a bike impervious to punctures, riders can ruin very important aspects of the machine's ride quality. A bike with nearly flat-proof tires will have much higher rolling resistance and will feel noticeably more sluggish than the same bike with regular tires. This can take a lot of the joy out of the ride.

Glass flats can be prevented somewhat by adjusting your route to avoid significant amounts of broken glass. Not all glass is created equal, however. Broken car windows rarely cause flats, because auto safety glass crumbles into dull-edged pebbles. Shards of bottle glass are the real problem. If you do ride through some bottle glass, it may be helpful to quickly wipe the tire using a *gloved* hand or your shoe. (Sometimes glass shards take their time cutting through the tire and tube.) This move takes a little practice to avoid putting said hand or shoe in the spokes—which would be a lot worse than a flat tire.

If you pick up a goathead thorn (much more common in certain areas of the country), tire-wiping probably won't do any good. Unlike glass, which can work its way slowly but steadily through the tire and tube, goatheads (aka puncture vine)

Goathead thorns are incredibly hard, akin to the hardest known hardwoods on the planet. Goathead spikes cut through tire and tube—even Kevlar strips—with the greatest of ease.

implant themselves to the hilt on first contact, typically breaking off the body of the thorn in the first few tire revolutions and leaving only the spike. The top of the spike may be visible in the tire, like a tiny, light-colored nail head.

Goathead punctures are largely avoidable due to the insidious nature of the thorn itself. These things are so efficient at sticking to tires and the soles of shoes that any well-traveled surface will be "cleaned" of thorns rather quickly. So simply confining your route to well-traveled surfaces is an easy and effective way to prevent thorn flats (and glass flats too, to some extent). Commuters get into trouble with thorns when they cut corners, ride through vacant lots, and ride at the very edge of bike paths and roads.

Riding over the parent plant, "Puncture Vine" (*Tribulus terrestris*), tends to result in a multi-thorn attack on both tires. This is . . . most unfortunate. Unless you have two spare tubes on board,

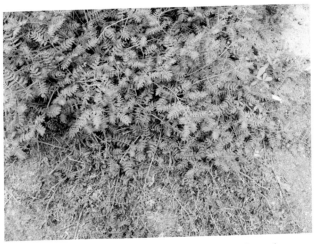

Tribulus terrestris (puncture vine) produces the insidious thorns that plague cyclists, primarily in Western states. Being able to recognize the plant will help you prevent goathead punctures.

the logistics involved in overcoming multiple thorn punctures are daunting. Most likely you will end up in a cab or searching out some other alternate means of transport. Learn what the evil weed looks like and where it likes to grow, and do your best to avoid it.

PRO TIP: If you do pick up a goathead, leaving it in the tire may be the best short-term strategy. The thorn provides the perfect custom-size plug for the hole it already made in your tire and tube. As long as the thorn remains implanted, the loss of air will be relatively slow. Pull the thing out and— *whoooooooosh!* So think twice before plucking that thorn out of the tire. It may be best to leave it in place and deal with the puncture after arriving at your destination.

If you ever get a puncture on the *under*side of a tube, it's most likely due to a problem with the rim strip. Rims are taped inside to keep the relatively sharp edges around the spoke holes from cutting the tube when inflated. But rim tape can go bad in a few different ways. Sometimes it gets moved aside just enough to reveal an edge. These flats are easily preventable by using good quality cloth rim strip that is wide enough to cover everything, even if it shifts a bit.

There is unfortunately another common type of puncture, which does not involve any sharp foreign objects penetrating the tube: the pinch flat, sometimes called the snakebite. Pinch flats occur when the wheel strikes an edge (of something or other) with enough force to bottom out the tire against the rim. When the tire and rim meet, the tube becomes collateral damage. These events usually result in two cuts in the tube, parallel to each other and about a centimeter apart. (Make sure you patch both holes, or cover both with one large patch.) The pinch flat is also easily preventable by keeping the tires well inflated and avoiding smashing into curbs, potholes, rocks in the road— you name it. Stop smashing. Or at least smash more delicately. Pinch flats can also be prevented by using tubeless tires, which have become common on mountain bikes. But that's a topic for another day.

Tires that are extremely worn start to look like swiss cheese. Eventually they allow the inner tube to pop out just enough to contact the street surface. If this happens, the tube will abrade quickly and "blow out." Replace seriously worn-out tires before they leave you frustrated on the side of the road. (*NOTE:* Blowouts aren't like punctures and may be difficult to repair. Flats caused by excess tire wear require the tire to be "booted," or the tube will be punctured repeatedly. The best "boot" material is a piece of rubber.)

PRO TIP: Carry a little roll of electrical tape with you. In cases of extreme tire wear, a strip of electrical tape inside the tire will extend tire life for a few more weeks. In the event of a puncture, this versatile item can help in many ways. If you don't have any patches left, electrical tape can be used like a stick-on patch to slow a leak to a manageable rate. A strip or two of electrical tape placed over the puncture *on the outside of the tire* **might even slow a leak enough to get you where you need to go, without even removing the wheel! If the rim strip has been compromised (another insidious source of flats), electrical tape will do the trick.**

A fair number of punctures are caused by something else altogether: the rider's failure to patch the tube correctly. Hopefully we can head those mistakes off at the pass in the following section.

REPAIRING FLAT TIRES

Experienced commuters usually prefer this method of repairing flat tires: Pull the offending article out of the tire, put in the spare tube that is always carried for such an occasion, air it up, and go. Then, if they feel like it, they can repair the old tube at their leisure and use it as a spare. This will save about 10 to 15 minutes over repairing the tube with a patch kit. However, complications may arise. What happens if you put in the new tube and then roll through another patch of thumbtacks? No matter how many extra tubes you carry, there will come a day when you need one more.

To commute with confidence, learn how to patch tubes in the field. The repair will require tire levers, a patch kit, a pump, and a little bit of finesse.

First, do a little recon. Inspect the outside of the tire and try to find out what caused the puncture and where it's located on

Insert a tire lever under the bead of the tire, and pry the tire over the lip of the rim. Be careful not to pinch the tube when you do this. PHOTO COURTESY SCOTT ADAMS © MORRIS BOOK PUBLISHING, LLC

the tire/tube. It might be pretty obvious. There might be a loud hiss emanating from the spot; there could even be an obvious thorn or other gremlin visible on the tire. Knowing this information will give you a good head start on fixing the flat, but it's not absolutely critical. We'll find that puncture one way or another.

Remove the wheel from the frame.

Using tire levers, remove one side of the tire from the rim. This takes a little practice, but it's not too difficult. With one lever, carefully (don't pinch the tube) pry the tire off the rim and hold it there by hooking the other end of the lever around a spoke. Then use a second lever to progressively pry the rest of one side of the tire off the rim. (I think the third lever in the set is a spare.)

Pull the tube out of the tire. It probably won't be necessary to remove it completely. Leave the valve stem in the rim unless the puncture is close to the valve stem.

Alternate tire levers, pulling the bead of the tire over the rim, section by section, until one side of the tire bead is completely off the rim. PHOTO COURTESY SCOTT ADAMS © MORRIS BOOK PUBLISHING, LLC

Thoroughly inspect the *inside of the tire,* and remove any protruding thorns, glass, tacks, staples, etc., noting their location. This check can be accomplished with bare fingers if you're careful about it. It's better to use some sort of soft cloth—hosiery may be ideal—and wipe it around the inside of the tire, feeling for snags. Performing this step at this point is helpful because any information you get about the number and location of

Remove the rest of the tire and tube from the rim. This can be done by hand. It's easiest to remove the valve stem last. PHOTO COURTESY SCOTT ADAMS © MORRIS BOOK PUBLISHING, LLC

punctures could make life easier as we go forward. (Note that this step won't necessarily provide all the information you need, because an item may fall out of the tire after it causes a puncture, leaving no trace other than the tiny hole.) Whether you do this now or later, do it sometime *before* you put the tube back in or you're likely to give yourself another puncture.

Locate the puncture on the tube. You may already have a good idea where it is, based on the location of the thorn or other sharp bit you found inside the tire. If not, pump up the tube a bit (say, twenty pumps) and listen for the telltale hiss. If you don't hear anything, pump up the tube some more. Very windy days, busy highways, loud downtown areas, and the like will make the task of listening for a puncture exceedingly difficult, if not impossible. If you're facing one or all of these challenges, try moving your flat-fixing operation to a sheltered, quiet area. If you pump up the tube and still can't hear anything, there is one

Wipe the inside of the tire to clean out any dirt, sand, glass, thorns, etc. Any of these may be the cause of your flat and will puncture the tire again if not removed. PHOTO COURTESY SCOTT ADAMS

more chance at finding the hole: Dunk the tube underwater bit by bit, and look for bubbles. Air bubbles are the final authority on the existence, or not, of any holes in the tube. But if the closest stoppable sink or pool of water is nowhere near, this method won't be much help to the deflated commuter.

Now that you've pinpointed the puncture, follow the directions in the patch kit to repair the tube. I recommend traditional style patch kits, which include a tube of bonding agent, patches, and a little sheet of sandpaper. Glueless patches are easier to use, but their performance is spotty at best. They may get you where you need to go, but the adhesive patches tend to fail before too long, which means you have to deal with the flat all over again. On the other hand, properly applied patches from a traditional kit will not fail—they may as well be part of the tube. (When I

Find the hole. To do this, pump air into the tube until you hear the *psssss* of air escaping. Hold your finger over the hole or mark it so that you don't lose it. PHOTO COURTESY SCOTT ADAMS © MORRIS BOOK PUBLISHING, LLC

worked as a messenger I used tubes with up to forty patches on them. Eventually the valve stem will go or the tube will fail in some other way, but the patches are never a problem.)

Repairing a puncture with a patch kit involves a few very important but seemingly arbitrary tasks. First, the area around the puncture (an area at least as large as the patch) must be roughed up thoroughly with the sandpaper in the kit. This is necessary to remove a nonstick chemical on the tube and is otherwise helpful in making the patch bond to the tube. Make sure to sand off all the little seams and ridges on the tube. A good patch job starts with a good sanding job.

Next apply a thin film of "glue" around the puncture. (This really isn't glue but a chemical bonding agent that works very differently than glue.) Again, the area covered by the bonding

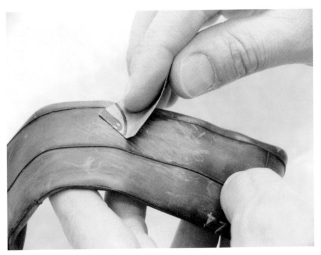

Rough up the area around the puncture with the sandpaper included in the kit, or the patch won't hold. This is a critical step to ensure proper glue adhesion. PHOTO COURTESY SCOTT ADAMS © MORRIS BOOK PUBLISHING, LLC

agent must be greater than the size of the patch; otherwise the edges of the patch won't stick and the patch will probably fail.

The next step should be the easiest. Although it's probably the most important step of all, somehow it remains the most mysterious and neglected step: Wait. Wait for the glue to dry completely. This should take about 5 or 10 minutes. Check the tackiness of the bonding agent with a fingernail. The lack of patience in most human flat-fixers won't allow them to wait long enough. Plus, they didn't read the directions and think they need to apply the patch before the glue dries. Consequently, their patches don't work. Wait. Be patient. Use the time productively: Make a phone call or perhaps visit the nearest drinking establishment in preparation for the workday. Don't worry about waiting too long—you can't. In fact, you could leave it to dry overnight and the patch would stick perfectly.

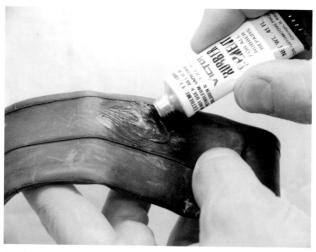

Apply a thin layer of glue to the sanded area. Allow the glue to dry completely (at least 5 minutes) before applying the patch.
PHOTO COURTESY SCOTT ADAMS © MORRIS BOOK PUBLISHING, LLC

Apply the patch firmly over the hole, pressing in place to ensure complete contact around the edges with the glue. PHOTO COURTESY SCOTT ADAMS © MORRIS BOOK PUBLISHING, LLC

Stuff the tube back into the tire. PHOTO COURTESY SCOTT ADAMS © MORRIS BOOK PUBLISHING, LLC

Beginning opposite the valve, use your thumbs to push the tire onto the rim. Be careful not to pinch the tube in between the tire and the rim. PHOTO COURTESY SCOTT ADAMS © MORRIS BOOK PUBLISHING, LLC

Fill the tire with air, checking to make sure the tube doesn't bulge from the rim; otherwise you could be in for a big bang. PHOTO COURTESY SCOTT ADAMS © MORRIS BOOK PUBLISHING, LLC

Press the patch on with a bit of force. Don't bother removing the cellophane cover if you don't want.

Stuff the repaired tube back into the tire, which has been thoroughly vetted for thorns and other sharp objects.

Roll the tire onto the rim. Unfortunately, this last step could be the most difficult and annoying one of all. Some tires and rims are more difficult to work with than others. In extreme cases, try using the outside of a shoe to lever the last bit of tire onto the rim. Make sure the tube isn't caught between the rim and tire. You may have to pause here and there to tuck the tube up into the tire with a tire lever.

Pump and roll.

When it all works out, the entire procedures takes about 15 minutes. That's probably faster than calling for a cab.

TRUING A WHEEL

Rims frequently get knocked a bit out of alignment due to striking the edges of potholes, curbs, or tracks; hitting rocks in the road; and other things like that. Just about any kind of crash or collision could bend one or both wheels. Spokes also break or loosen over time, which will also cause the rim to twist "out of true."

Most moderate bends in the rim can be fixed or at least improved with a simple tool—the spoke wrench. Take a close look at the wheel. Notice how some of the spokes reach from the rim to one side of the hub and some attach to the other side. When you tighten a spoke (by twisting the spoke nipple with a spoke wrench), you pull the rim toward that side of the hub. When you loosen a spoke, you allow the rim to pull away from that side of the hub. It's really pretty simple. Locate the portion of the rim that is bent out of alignment, perhaps by turning the bike over and watching the rim spin past the brake pads. Then use subtle tightening/loosening of the spokes in the vicinity of the bend to coax the rim back into alignment. Just a quarter turn of the spoke wrench can make a significant difference, so use a light touch.

Perhaps the trickiest part of the whole thing is figuring out which direction to turn the wrench. When looking at the top of the rim (the surface closest to the hub and farthest from the tire), twisting the spoke nipple counterclockwise tightens the spoke.

Tightening a spoke not only pulls the rim laterally in that direction but also pulls it *down* toward the hub. To keep a rim round, then, as well as straight, truing should involve a combination of tightening and loosening nearby spokes. Also, be careful not to overtighten any spoke, as this could crack the rim.

Keep in mind that rims also twist themselves moderately out of alignment when they are cracked and ready to fail, so be sure to inspect a bent rim closely to ensure that the wheel will be safe to use, straight or not. Look for bulges in the rim sidewall and/or hairline cracks in the sidewall parallel to the circumference of the rim. Usually a cracked sidewall makes itself apparent when braking, as the pads bump over the bulge in the rim. (*NOTE:* This only applies to traditional rim brakes. If you're using some other kind of brake, such as disc, you won't be able to feel a bulge in the sidewall. But the rim sidewall is unlikely to crack in the first place, because this failure is associated with excess sidewall wear due to braking.)

If the rim is so badly warped that the wheel has taken on the general appearance of a potato chip, it's probably a goner. (Strangely enough, this has long been known as "pretzeling" a wheel. Clearly it should be called "potato chipping.") However, it may be possible to straighten a very bent wheel just enough to make it rideable by slamming it hard on the ground, preferably against the installed and inflated tire rather than the bare rim. If you need to try this last-ditch method, use just enough violence to bend the rim back toward true (violence is probably what took it out, after all), but not enough to ruin it. Oh, and make sure you remove the wheel from the bike first! Then use the spoke wrench to pull it further into alignment. A lot of desperate riders have enabled their potato-chipped wheels to roll, just barely, using this method.

Bicycle wheels (comprising the rim, spokes, and hub) are an amazing bit of nineteenth-century technology. With proper maintenance and a little attention with the spoke wrench, a basic, well-built tangentially spoked wheel will carry you reliably year after year. Usually it takes a crash to end a wheel's service life. There are good reasons bike wheels have been built that way for so long. Problems start to arise when non-racers get cute with radial spoke patterns and low-spoke-count wheels.

THE DRIVETRAIN

Many rides have been spoiled, or at least complicated, by poorly functioning drivetrains. At their worst, malfunctioning drivetrains become a legitimate danger. Fortunately, most problems in this area are fixed easily with a few simple tools and some lubricant.

Lubrication is one of the most basic and important aspects of bike maintenance. The chain is the most lube-thirsty component on the entire bike. Keep the chain well lubed by regularly dripping one of a multitude of suitable products on every link. Wipe the excess. Well-lubed pulleys, derailleur pivots, and cables are also necessary for smooth drivetrain function. Cable friction is an insidious wrecker of drivetrain function; it's surprisingly noisy as well. Pay special attention to any cable guides under the bottom bracket—ground zero for mud and moisture.

During and after a big rainstorm, you might notice that all the little creaks and groans your bike used to make have been silenced—the rainwater has temporarily lubed the machine's innumerable nooks and crannies. But water is a solvent, and when the bike dries out, a lot of the lubrication that had been on the drivetrain will have been removed, leaving you with a creaking, squealing rattletrap. Make sure to lubricate the drivetrain especially well after any wet rides.

Drivetrains wear in a distinctive fashion. As you put in the miles, the chain "stretches." It doesn't really stretch but elongates due to wear and loosening at the pivot points. As the chain wears, the teeth of the chainrings and cogs also wear. Eventually each gear tooth will assume a lopsided shark-fin profile.

There are two major schools of thought on chain replacement. Traditionally, well-heeled cyclists are taught to replace the chain on a fairly frequent basis because the chainrings and cogset will also have to be replaced if the chain has elongated beyond a certain point. (It is commonly advised that the chain should be replaced if twelve 1-inch links measure $\frac{1}{16}$ inch beyond 1 foot. If the formerly 1-foot section of chain has elongated by $\frac{1}{8}$ inch, it's too late to replace only the chain. The whole she-bang—chain, cogset, and chainrings—needs to be replaced.) A new chain won't mesh with overly worn-out gear teeth. Others just use the old chain until it's exhausted and the gears are so worn that the chain starts to skip over them, then replace everything all at once. In the end, these two methods seem to work out about the same in terms of expense and energy expended.

ADJUSTING THE DRIVETRAIN

If the bike's not shifting quite right, everything's *well lubricated* (excess friction in the cable housing is the most likely culprit when it comes to shifting problems), and the derailleur hanger isn't bent, the derailleur is probably out of adjustment. The first and best way to adjust your bike's shifting is to twist one of the barrel adjusters on the rear derailleur cable counterclockwise to pull up the slack in the cable. There are probably two of these barrel adjusters on your bike—one at the derailleur and one at the down tube cable boss or at the shifter, depending on whether you have roadie shifters or flat bar shifters. This is one of the easiest and most effective adjustments and one that can be performed while riding, which is something we can't say very often.

Adjust the limit screws on the derailleur if the chain is shifting off the cassette on either side. Unfortunately, this adjustment cannot be performed while riding and usually requires a small Phillips-head screwdriver.

A third adjustment screw on the derailleur sets the distance between the top pulley and the cassette. If this distance is set too short, the pulley and the largest cog will touch and the drivetrain won't function properly; if set too long, shifting will feel tight and sluggish.

CHAINLINE

Take care not to "cross the chain" too severely. For instance, when the chain is on the biggest chainring in front and the largest cog in the rear, you can look down and see that it's angled acutely out of alignment. The chain has to reach from the extreme outside position in front to the extreme inside position in back. You may hear a lot of extra noise coming from the drivetrain that seems impossible to adjust away. It may be difficult or impossible to shift. This bad chainline causes extra wear on the chain, chainring, cog, and derailleur. Especially avoid using the large chainring–largest cog combination, in which the chain is not only out of alignment but also stretched to the max, because you'll sacrifice the derailleur hanger on the frame if the chain isn't long enough to be forced into that position. The combo of small chainring (closest to the bike) and small cog (farthest from the bike) could give the drivetrain a lot of unnecessary difficulty as well. When beginner bicyclists take their bikes to the shop, unable to get the derailleurs adjusted without audible rubbing and difficult shifting, it is very often the result of misunderstanding the limitations of the equipment and trying to jam their bike into one of these extreme gear combinations.

When it's all said and done, an eighteen-speed bike might only offer fourteen or fifteen usable gears. Don't worry though—it is highly unlikely that you will need more than a handful of them on your commute.

ADJUSTING THE BRAKES

These days, bicycles can be equipped with several different types of brakes. Brake adjustment is a little bit outside the scope of this book, but there are a few easy tricks that can be performed with an Allen wrench in the middle of a commute, if necessary.

Disc brakes are becoming common on road-worthy commuter bikes and may be hydraulic or cable-actuated. Disk brake calipers sometimes need realignment. This is an easy fix. Simply loosen the bolts attaching the caliper to the frame or fork, clamp the brake to center the caliper, then tighten the bolts with the brake clamped. If the piston isn't retracting all the way back into the caliper (a common problem), remove the wheel, then use a large flat-head screwdriver to forcefully wedge the piston all the way back. Keep the pads on when you do this. Any more adjustment than that will probably involve bleeding the hydraulic lines, which is not a roadside repair.

Rim brakes come in a few different subtypes but are almost always cable-actuated. It may be possible to fix mushy-feeling, weak cable-actuated brakes by loosening the cable anchor bolt and pulling a little (if not tiny) bit of cable through, then retightening. Also, check the alignment of the pads as they hit the rim. As brake pads wear, they tend to "dive" under the rim. Loosen the bolt and realign the pad, making sure it doesn't rub on the tire. Replace worn pads before you get metal-on-metal contact. Commuters who ride through a lot of wet or slushy conditions should stow an extra set of brake pads in their backpack or panniers. Also remember that the proper function of rim brakes depends on the condition of the rim. If the rim is bent, the brakes will function poorly, perhaps dangerously.

CONCLUSION: THANK YOU

In time you will find the unsteadiness and general cluelessness with which you started bicycle commuting replaced by a genuine confidence that is derived from true experience. You'll start to develop your own unique solutions to all the problems mentioned in this guide. When your coworkers start asking you for bike-commuting advice, you'll know you're on the right track.

Thank you for reading this book, and thank you for commuting by bike.

APPENDIX: Resources

For step-by-step repair instructions and other detailed mechanical information, see www.sheldonbrown.com and www.park tool.com.

For links to local bicycle laws and advocacy organizations, and research on bicycle accidents and injuries, patterns of use, bicycle facilities, and helmet effectiveness, check out www.industrializedcyclist.com/lies.html.

Other great resources include:

Andrews, Guy. *Mountain Bike Maintenance.* Guilford, CT: FalconGuides, 2006.

———. *Road Bike Maintenance.* Guilford, CT: FalconGuides, 2008.

Hurst, Robert. *The Art of Cycling.* Guilford, CT: FalconGuides, 2006.

———. *The Cyclist's Manifesto.* Guilford, CT: FalconGuides, 2009.

Stuhaug, Dennis. *Basic Essentials Bicycle Touring.* Guilford, CT: FalconGuides, 2006.

GLOSSARY

Derailleur: The cable-actuated mechanism that moves the chain from one sprocket to another.

Dooring: A type of collision in which a bicyclist collides with a suddenly opened car door.

Door Zone: The area next to parked cars in which a cyclist is very vulnerable to colliding with a suddenly opened car door.

Draft: *v.* To ride in the slipstream of another rider or vehicle.

Drops: The lower section of the curved road handlebar that offers the most aerodynamic hand position.

Chainline: The angle of the chain when seen from above.

Chainring: The front sprocket(s).

Clipless pedal: A type of pedal that is used in conjunction with a special cleat and shoe. The name is derived from its lack of toeclip.

Cogset: The collection of sprockets at the rear hub.

Cyclocross: A mutant discipline of bicycle racing that is really, really hard to explain. Strongly associated with Belgians.

Filter: *v.* To ride past a line of cars at a traffic light or stop sign.

Freewheel: A mechanism that enables a bicycle to coast.

Looked-but-failed-to-see error: A type of crash in which a vehicle operator fails to notice another road user and collides with him or her. The most common type of car-bike crash.

Pannier: A bag that attaches to a rack and hangs beside the bike's wheel, front or back. Typically used for touring or commuting.

Peloton: A pack of riders in a race.

Right hook: A type of collision in which a car turns right and hits a cyclist going straight.

Sharrow: An on-street marking that combines an arrow and a bicycle; designed to provoke awareness in cyclists as well as drivers.

Semi-slick: A tire with a small amount of tread.

Slick: A tire with no tread.

Spin: *v.* To pedal at high revolutions per minute (rpm's).

Standover: The distance from the ground to the top of the bicycle frame. Should be shorter than the distance from the ground to your crotch.

Tire lever: A tool used to take a tire off of the rim. Usually sold in threes.

Toe clip: A device that can be attached to a pedal that holds the shoe more securely. Usually used in conjunction with an adjustable strap.

Track stand: The act of balancing a bike at zero velocity. So named because of its origins in bicycle track racing.

True: *v.* To straighten, as in a wheel. *n.* Straight.

Tubular: An old-school type of tire that is glued onto the rim. Used almost exclusively for racing.

BIBLIOGRAPHY

City of Boulder, Transportation Division. *Safe Streets Boulder: A Study of Motor Vehicle Collisions Involving Bicyclists and Pedestrians.* February 2012.

City of Madison, Traffic Engineering Division. *2010 Crash Report*; www.cityofmadison.com/trafficEngineering/documents/Reports-Studies/CrashReports/2010_CrashReport.pdf.

Hoehner, Christine, Carolyn Barlow, Peg Allen & Mario Schootman. "Commuting Distance, Cardiorespiratory Fitness, and Metabolic Risk," *American Journal of Preventive Medicine,* June 2012, pp. 571–78.

Hurst, Robert. *The Art of Cycling.* Guilford, CT: FalconGuides, 2006.

Idaho Office of Highway Safety. Idaho Traffic Crashes 2010, p. 60; http://itd.idaho.gov/ohs/2010Data/Analysis2010.pdf.

League of American Bicyclists. "2010 Bicycle Commuting Data Released"; www.bikeleague.org/news/acs2010.php.

Wessels, Ralph L. "Bicycle Collisions in Washington State: A Six-Year Perspective, 1988–1993," *Transportation Research Record 1538,* pp. 81–90.

Wolf, Randall. "Cyclist Says 3 Foot Law Ignored By Cars, Cops," *Nyack News & Views,* July 9, 2012; www.nyacknewsandviews.com/2012/07/rwolf_biking3ftlaw/.

Zaleski, Andrew. "Study Finds Three-Foot Law Not Followed," *Urbanite,* April 16, 2012; www.urbanitebaltimore.com/StaffReport/archives/2012/04/16/study-finds-three-foot-law-not-followed.

INDEX

ABOUT THE AUTHOR

Robert Hurst is a true bicycle lover and a longtime student of the dance of traffic. His book *The Art of Cycling* is acknowledged by experts to be the most complete, realistic, and readable source available for information and tips about cycling in traffic.

Robert has also written *The Art of Mountain Biking: Single-track Skills for All Riders, Mountain Biking Colorado's San Juan Mountains: Durango and Telluride, Road Biking Colorado's Front Range,* and *The Cyclist's Manifesto,* all for FalconGuides.

He currently lives in Denver, Colorado, with his wife, who is also a bicyclist, and his newborn daughter, Beatrice, a cat, and two dogs, who are not.